The Grammar of Spelling Grade 2

by B.J. Loyd

Resources for Reading Comprehension, Writing, and Spelling

C080	Imitation in Writing: Aesop's Fables
C083	Imitation in Writing: Fairy Tales
C084	Imitation in Writing: Medieval Legends
C085	Imitation in Writing: Greek Myths
C086	Imitation in Writing: Greek Heroes
C087	Imitation in Writing: Poetry
C088	Imitation in Writing: Poetry - Teacher's Edition
C089	Imitation in Writing: Poetry Primer
C089TE	Imitation in Writing: Poetry Primer - Teacher's Edition
C090	Reading Comprehension: Beginning Literature 1
C092	Reading Comprehension: Beginning Literature 2
C093	Reading Comprehension: Stories from Grandma's Attic
C094	Reading Comprehension: More Stories from Grandma's Attic
C096	Reading Comprehension: Still More Stories from Grandma's Attic
C098	Reading Comprehension: Little House in the Big Woods
C099	Reading Comprehension: On the Banks of Plum Creek
C100	Reading Comprehension: Little House on the Prairie
C102	Reading Comprehension: By the Shores of Silver Lake
C104	Reading Comprehension: The Long Winter
C106	Reading Comprehension: Charlotte's Web
C107	Reading Comprehension: The Lion, the Witch, and the Wardrobe
C108	Reading Comprehension: The Horse and His Boy
C109	Reading Comprehension: The Magician's Nephew
C110	Reading Comprehension: Prince Caspian
C111	Reading Comprehension: The Silver Chair
C112	Reading Comprehension: The Voyage of The Dawn Treader
C113	Reading Comprehension: The Last Battle
C116	Writing Trails with Great Composers
C117	Writing Trails with Men of Science
C118	Immigrant Trails in American History
C119	Writing Trails in American History
C120	Tales from Shakespeare
C133	Grammar of Spelling/Grade 3
C134	Grammar of Spelling/Grades 4-6
C140	Upper Grammar Literature Book I
C141	Upper Grammar Literature Book II
C142	Upper Grammar Literature Book III
C143	Upper Grammar Literature Book IV
C144	Upper Grammar Literature Book V
C330	Reading with Purpose

C132 Grammar of Spelling/Grade 2
ISBN 1-930443-64-1

Logos School Materials
110 Baker Street
Moscow, Idaho 83843
Call (208) 883-3199 or 866-562-2174
for a free catalog

The Grammar of Spelling

The Art of Reading and Writing English

by Isaac Watts

The Knowledge of letters is one of the greatest blessings that ever God bestowed on the children of men. By this means we preserve for our own use, through all our lives, what our memory would have lost in a few days, and lay up rich treasure of knowledge for those that shall come after us.

By the arts of reading and writing, we can sit at home and acquaint ourselves what is done in all the distant parts of the world, and find what our fathers did long ago in the first ages of mankind. By this means a Briton holds correspondence with his friend in America or Japan, and manages all his traffic. We learn by this means how the old Romans lived, how the Jews worshiped: We learn what Moses wrote, what Enoch prophesied, where Adam dwelt, and what he did soon after the creation; and those who shall live when the Day of Judgement comes, may learn by the same means what we now speak, and what we do in Great-Britain, or in the land of China.

In short, the art of letters does, as it were, revive all the past ages of men, and set them at once upon the stage; and brings all the nations from afar, and gives them, as it were, a general interview: so that the most distant nations, and distant ages of mankind may converse together, and grow into acquaintance.

But the greatest blessing of all, is the knowledge of the Holy Scripture, wherein God has appointed his servants in ancient times to write down the discoveries which he has made of his power and justice, His providence and grace, that we who live near the end of time may learn the way to heaven and everlasting happiness.

Thus letters give us a sort of immortality in this world, and they are given us in the Word of God to support our immortal hopes in the next.

Those therefore who willfully neglect this sort of knowledge, and despise the art of letters, need no heavier curse of punishment than what they choose for themselves, to live and die in ignorance both of the things of God and man.

If the terror of such a thought, will not awaken the slothful to seek so much acquaintance with their mother-tongue, as may render them capable of some of the advantages here described; I know not where to find a persuasive that shall work upon souls, that are sunk down so far into brutal stupidity, and so unworthy of a reasonable nature.

2nd Grade Spelling

Children in the Grammar stage love knowledge and facts. They are fascinated by words, and they can memorize easily. Spelling correctly is a "tool" we want to give the students that will help them with written communication.

Spelling is a discipline. It is hard work. This spelling program lacks pretty pictures and the fluff of other programs on the market. The no-nonsense worksheets that accompany each lesson are basically an exercise in rewriting the spelling words many times. Spelling, for the second grade student, concentrates on *hearing* each part of the basic root word. The student works primarily with a foundation, using the building blocks of reading and phonics. However, this approach is not a reading-spelling program with 29 or 30 spelling or phonics rules for the students to memorize. It is a program of *hearing* blends, clusters and vowel sounds, memorizing words, and being able to spell dictated words and sentences. The emphasis is on the words themselves. The strength of this spelling program is the cumulative spelling lists and dictation.

Word lists for the 2nd Grade:

1. Word families (old, cold, sold, hold, told, bold, light, might, fright, mightily...)

2. Sight words (come, they, done, friend, because, was, really...)

3. Compound words (toothbrush, softball, driveway, sunset...)

4. Number words (one through twenty)

5. Color words

6. Days of the week and months of the year

7. Contractions

8. Homophones (hear, here, to, two, too, wood, would, there, their, they're...)

9. The teacher's name

10. The student's complete name, full address, and complete phone number

11. Common suffixes added to base words (s, es, ed, ing, er, est...)

The Grammar of Spelling
Contents

Page

6		Features of the 36 Lessons
8		Sample Worksheet 2
9		How to Use 2nd Grade Grammar of Spelling
10	Lesson & Test 1	Introductory Lesson
11	Lesson & Test 2	Short CVC Words
12	Lesson & Test 3	Initial Blend CCVC Words
13	Lesson & Test 4	Initial Blend CCVC Words
14	Lesson & Test 5	Initial Blend CCVC and CCCVC Words
15	Lesson & Test 6	Final Blend CVCC and CCVCC Words
16	Lesson & Test 7	Review Words
17	Lesson & Test 8	Final Blend CVCC and CCVCC Words
18	Lesson & Test 9	Final Blends **ng**, **nk**
19	Lesson & Test 10	Final Endings **ff**, **ll**, **ss**, **zz**
20	Lesson & Test 11	Number Words (one through ten)
21	Lesson & Test 12	Beginning Sound <u>**a**</u> Words, **al** Words, **wa** Words
22	Lesson & Test 13	Review Sight Words and New Sight Words
23	Lesson & Test 14	Money Words and "**o**" says short /ŭ/
24	Lesson & Test 15	Review Words
25	Lesson & Test 16	Two Syllable Words
26	Lesson & Test 17	Vowel-consonant-e
27	Lesson & Test 18	Diphthong **i**, **y** says /ī/
28	Lesson & Test 19	Diphthong **a**
29	Lesson & Test 20	Diphthong **e**
30	Lesson & Test 21	Review Words
31	Lesson & Test 22	Diphthong **e**, Diphthong **o**, **y** says /ē/
32	Lesson & Test 23	Diphthong **o**, Diphthong **u**, Soft **c** Words
33	Lesson & Test 24	Diphthong **oo**
34	Lesson & Test 25	Diphthong **oo**, Diphthong **ô**, Soft **c** Words
35	Lesson & Test 26	Diphthong **ou**, Hard **c** Words, Consonant <u>le</u> Syllable Words
36	Lesson & Test 27	Review Words
37	Lesson & Test 28	Diphthong **oi** and Consonant <u>le</u> Syllable Words
38	Lesson & Test 29	Diphthong **er** and Consonant <u>le</u> Syllable Words
39	Lesson & Test 30	Diphthong **er,** Complete Address & Phone Number
40	Lesson & Test 31	Days of the Week, Color Words, Address & Phone Number
41	Lesson & Test 32	Months of the Year, Address & Phone Number
42	Lesson & Test 33	Review Words
43	Lesson & Test 34	**tch**, **g**, **dge**, **and** <u>r-controlled</u> Words
44	Lesson & Test 35	Number Words (eleven through twenty) and Contractions
45	Lesson & Test 36	Review Words
47		Master List of Spelling Words
53		Worksheets for Weekly Lessons

Features of the 36 Lessons

WORD BOXES:

The spelling words are arranged in word boxes and review word boxes which are found on pages 45 through 50. These may be copied and sent home each week for study purposes.

The words are taught by a cumulative method. Each week the students are given a word box containing 20 to 24 new words. Past spelling words are put in a review word box. These words may show up on the spelling test, so the students need to remember how to spell them. After the accumulation of about 120 words, the review box is wiped clean of all but the sight words. Many high-use words will continue to show up on the spelling tests.

LESSONS:

Information is given about each lesson and instructions on what to teach are presented. Introduce the new spelling words and discuss the meaning of those words. Demonstrate family relationships, if possible. Emphasize *hearing* each sound in words. Orally discuss exceptions, sight words, meaning of homophones, and the adding of prefixes and suffixes.

Extra words are provided for dictation and practice. These words can be used for whole class or individual instruction, and they can be spelled orally or written.

WORKSHEETS:

Help the students identify the particular pattern or patterns for each week's words. The worksheets have four remaining parts. These may be completed on different days of the week or completed all in one day.

1. Repeat and Write: In this activity the teacher says the spelling word, the students listen, repeat the word in unison, and then write the word on the blank in print.

2. Alphabetize in Print or Cursive: The students are to alphabetize the words in groups and then use print or cursive to write the words on the blank. If they write the alphabetized number in the small circle provided, and copy the words only after the entire list is numbered, mistakes can be corrected easily. For example in Lesson #2 the students are to find the word that comes first alphabetically. This word is *cab.* Therefore in the circle to the right of the word *cab* the student is to write the number one. The number two will be written in the circle following the word *got* and so forth. This activity should be done together as a whole class led by the teacher for the first few weeks until the students understand how to alphabetize using the circles correctly.

3. Flip and Write: The students will look carefully at the word on the front of the sheet, keep the spelling in mind, flip the paper over and write the word in print or cursive on the blank. Do not allow the students to fold their papers and copy without flipping.

4. CAPITAL PRINT: The students are to carefully and neatly print each spelling word in capital letters. This provides an opportunity to see the words in a different format than usual, requiring more care and checking to insure that the words are indeed spelled correctly.

DICTATION:

Cumulative spelling lists and dictation are the heart of this spelling program. Dictation helps the students hear and write sentences. It reinforces listening and following directions skills. Words and sentences are provided for practice during the week and for the weekly test.

Each sentence should be dictated as you have the students' undivided attention. Say the sentence; repeat the sentence. Have the students repeat the sentence back two times. Dictate the sentence once more, and then the students may write it. Allow enough time for them to write the sentence. Finally, dictate the sentence again so they may check their work. <u>Proper capitalization and punctuation should be required and graded whenever the students write a sentence.</u>

**The teacher may need to spell some of the words in the sentences for the students. These words will be <u>underlined.</u>

TESTS:

First, students should write their name and write **Spelling Test** as the heading. Next, have the students fold their papers in half lengthwise and reopen the paper. The students should number their paper 1-10 along the side and 11-20 along the middle fold line, making sure they skip lines. They should do this every week, no matter how many words are used for the test. Numbers for dictated sentences will be written later as needed.

When giving the test, state the number and the word. Give a sentence using the word. <u>Repeat the word one time only</u>. Give the students ample time to write and then move on to the next word. Do not go back over the words. The students can and must learn to listen and spell promptly.

After giving the spelling words, have the students write the two sentences you dictate to them. Follow the same procedure for the test as you did during the practice lesson. (See the above directions.)

Each word on the test paper must be spelled correctly. Capitals and punctuation in sentences count equal to spelling words. (That's integration!) However, it is for you to decide if you want crossing t's and dotting i's and j's to be counted as making the word wrong or counted as one point off.

Sample Worksheet 2   Name_____ **Sally**_____
What is the pattern? __short CVC words__

Repeat and Write		Alphabetize in Print or Cursive
1. jam	___jăm_____ (3)	1. ____cab_____
2. set	___sĕt_____ (5)	2. ____got_____
3. got	___gŏt_____ (2)	3. ____jam_____
4. cab	___căb_____ (1)	4. ____met_____
5. met	___mĕt_____ (4)	5. ____set_____

6. sit	___sĭt_____ (4)	1. ____bug_____
7. bug	___bŭg_____ (1)	2. ____hum_____
8. win	___wĭn_____ (5)	3. ____pen_____
9. pen	___pĕn_____ (3)	4. ____sit_____
10. hum	___hŭm_____ (2)	5. ____win_____

11. nut	___nŭt_____ (4)	1. ____box_____
12. pin	___pĭn_____ (5)	2. ____has_____
13. box	___bŏx_____ (1)	3. ____log_____
14. log	___lŏg_____ (3)	4. ____nut_____
15. has	___hăs_____ (2)	5. ____pin_____

In the left hand column mark the short vowels with a breve.

Write your teacher's name. _____Mrs. Jordan _____

Worksheet 2-B   Name __ **Sally** _____

Flip and Write		CAPITAL PRINT	
1.	___jam_____	1.	____JAM_____
2.	___set_____	2.	____SET_____
3.	___got_____	3.	___GOT_____
4.	___cab_____	4.	___CAB _____
5.	___met_____	5.	___MET_____
6.	___sit_____	6.	___SIT_____
7.	___bug_____	7.	___BUG_____
8.	___win_____	8.	___WIN____
9.	___pen_____	9.	___PEN____
10.	___hum_____	10.	___HUM_____
11.	___nut_____	11.	___NUT_____
12.	___pin_____	12.	___PIN____
13.	___box_____	13.	___BOX____
14.	___log_____	14.	___LOG_____
15.	___has_____	15.	___HAS_____

Write: your first name   your middle name   your last name

_____ Sally _____   _____Ann _____   _____ Brown _____

   spelling   test   said   was   because

____ spelling ____   __ test ____   ___said___   __ was __   ____ because __

How to Use 2nd Grade Grammar of Spelling

Homework

Word Boxes: Send the new and review spelling boxes home on Monday or the previous Friday.

Monday (30 to 60 minutes)

Preview Time: Introduce the new spelling words and discuss the meaning of those words. Demonstrate family relationships, if possible. Emphasize *hearing* each sound in the word. Orally discuss exceptions, sight words, meanings of homophones, and the adding of prefixes and suffixes. This preview time will be as exciting and interesting to the students as you make it.

Dictation: Using the left column of the worksheet dictate each word to the students. They are to listen, repeat the word in unison, and then print the word on the blank.

Worksheet: The students may complete one side or both sides of the worksheet. They may do this after dictation or as a seatwork assignment during the day.

Tuesday (30 minutes)

Dictation: Dictate sentences to the students. Each sentence should be dictated as you have the students' undivided attention. Say the sentence; repeat the sentence. Have the students repeat the sentence back two times. Dictate the sentence once more, and then the students may write it. Allow enough time for them to write the sentence. Finally, dictate the sentence again so they may check their work. Correct the sentences by having the students cross out all misspelled words with one line (not erasing) and write the words correctly above. Send the sentence dictation paper home so the parents are aware of areas where they may help their child.

Wednesday (30 minutes)

Dictation: Dictate words from the new spelling list, from the extra words provided with each lesson, and from review word boxes.

Worksheet: The students may complete the worksheet, if they haven't done so yet.

Thursday and Friday (30 minutes each)

Testing: Give two spelling tests each week and record test scores for both. If a student gets 100% on Thursday, he does not have to take Friday's test and gets an automatic 100% for it. Students love this reward for hard work and a job well done. Usually the grades drastically improve for the second test. Friday's test does not have to be the same words. You, as the teacher, may want to change the test words.

Integration

Using the "tool": Expect and require the students to apply correct spelling to their other work as well. Require them to copy correctly.

Challenge students that get test marks of 100% three times in a row. Consider giving them "stella or star" words to learn each week. These stella words should come from your other studies.

Lesson 1 – Introductory Lesson

(The student's full name) _____
(The teacher's name) _____
    <u>Sight words</u>: spelling test said was they are of off because

DIRECTIONS:
    The student is to learn how to spell his/her <u>complete name</u> and the <u>teacher's name</u>. The names must be spelled with the proper capitals and punctuation marks.
    <u>Spelling</u> and <u>test</u> are to be memorized and are required as headings on each spelling test paper throughout the year.
    <u>Said, was, they, are, of, off,</u> and <u>because</u> are the first sight words to be taught and memorized.
    Introduce each word in the spelling box and explain how to spell it by stressing the initial and final blends (two or more consonants together), the vowel sounds, and how to add the suffixes. Explain the meaning of each word.
Beginning with the first lesson, the students need to be taught how to put their spelling words in alphabetical order. They will be required to do it every week.

EXTRA WORDS:
spell spelled   speller

DICTATION SENTENCES: You may have to spell the underlined words for the students.
(Student's name) can spell.
The spelling test was fun.
They spelled the <u>word</u> off because (teacher's name) said to spell off.
He will do a test of spelling.
I said we are <u>good</u> spellers.

TEST 1: 38 points

Spelling Test	Name	(3 pts.)
1. Teacher's name (Mrs. Jordan)	11. Student's first name	
2. they	12. Student's middle name (may be blank)	
3. off	13. Student's last name	
4. spelling	14.	(13 pts.)
5. was	15.	
6. of	16.	
7. said	17.	
8. test	18.	
9. are	19.	
10. because	20.	

21. They spell because because (Mrs. Jordan) said to spell because.   (15 pts.)
22. The spelling test was fun.   (7 pts.)

Lesson 2 – Short CVC Words

> **Pattern-CVC words**: jam set sit got hum cab net win box bug
> has pen pin log nut   **Sight words**: spelling test said was because

DIRECTIONS:

Review: The student's complete name and the teacher's name, spelling, test, said, was, they, are, of, off, because.

New Words: Introduce each CVC word (consonant, vowel, consonant) in the spelling box and explain how to spell it by stressing the consonants, the vowel sound, and how to double the final consonant to add suffixes. Explain the meaning of each word.

Show the students how to mark above the short vowel sound with a **breve (ŏ)** . A breve is an upward curved mark shaped like the smile on a smiley face.

Dictate many of the extra words below and have students orally spell the words.
Each week the extra words can be orally discussed, defined, memorized by the students, used for dictation in sentences and in spelling bees, or used for spelling tests.

EXTRA WORDS:

hat wet hit dot cut pat bed dim top mud sad pet tip hop hug ran ten him pot dug tap net mix hot run had red hid dog pup

DICTATION SENTENCES: You may have to spell underlined words for the students.
She has the jam and nuts.
Did you sit on the pin?
The bug ran up the log and met a dog.
He set the pen in the box.
I will win the spelling test.
He got to hum today.

TEST 2: 43 points

Spelling Test		Name	(3 pts.)
1. because	11. jam		
2. cab	12. pin		
3. set	13. met		
4. win	14. test		(20 pts.)
5. pen	15. hum		
6. box	16. sit		
7. spelling	17. was		
8. nut	18. got		
9. log	19. said		
10. has	20. bug		

21. Did you sit on the pin?   (8 pts.)
22. The bug ran up the log and met a dog.   (12 pts.)

Lesson 3 – Initial Blend CCVC Words

> **Pattern-CCVC words:** chop chin shed shut that them when whip blot
> blab clap club flag flip glad glob plan plus sled slim
> <u>Sight words:</u> you your says goes does

DIRECTIONS:

Review: Words from lessons 1 and 2

New Words: This lesson is the first group of words stressing initial consonant blends. These CCVC words start with 10 different blends: ch - sh - th - wh - bl - cl - fl - gl - pl - sl. There are five new sight words. Introduce each word in the spelling box and explain how to spell it by stressing the initial blend, the vowel sound, and how to add suffixes. Explain the meaning of each word.

Show the students how to mark above the short vowel sound with a **breve** (ă). A breve is an upward curved mark shaped like the smile on a smiley face.

Dictate many of the extra words below and have students orally spell the words.

EXTRA WORDS:

chap chat chip ship shop shot than then this thus whim bled clam
 clip clog flap flat glen plot plug plum slam slat slid slip

E. DICTATION SENTENCES:

Did you say your sled was in the shed?
When will the flag flip?
The club and whip <u>were</u> in your plan.
Does your chin look slim?
You will shut the flap on the ship.
Did we plan to get a plum and a clam?
They are glad that chap will blab.
We shot the flat chip off of the plug.

TEST 3: 47 points

Spelling Test	Name	(3 pts.)
1. does	11. chin	
2. flip	12. shut	
3. glad	13. plus	
4. that	14. glob	(20 pts.)
5. slim	15. flag	
6. blab	16. because *	
7. of *	17. was *	
8. clap	18. chop	
9. blot	19. said *	
10. goes	20. them	

The * denotes review words.

21. They had a club and a whip in the plan.   (12 pts.)
22. When did you say your sled was in the shed?   (12 pts.)

Lesson 4 – Initial Blend CCVC Words

> **Pattern-CCVC words:** brim   brag   crab   crop   drum   drop   fret   from   grin
> grab   prop   prim   trip   trot   scab   scan   skid   skin   smog   smug
> <u>Sight words:</u> where   were   have   there   here

DIRECTIONS:

Review: Words from lessons 1, 2, and 3.

New Words: This lesson is another group of words stressing initial consonant blends. These CCVC words start with 10 different blends: br - cr - dr - fr - gr - pr - tr - sc - sk - sm. There are five new sight words. Introduce each word in the spelling box and explain how to spell it by stressing the initial blend and the vowel sound. Explain the meaning of each word.

Show the students how to mark above the short vowel sound with a breve.

Dictate many of the extra words below and have students orally spell the words.

EXTRA WORDS:

brat   bran   crib   drab   drip   drag   frog   grub   grip   trim   trip
scat   scum   skim   skip   skit

DICTATION SENTENCES:

Did he grab the scab on your skin?
She will be a crab and fret on the trip.
He will trot from here to there.
I said you look smug and prim.
Do not grin and brag <u>about</u> your drum.
The crab said scat to the frog.
I will grab the grub and skip in the skit.
Where were you <u>going</u> to drag your sled?

TEST 4: 47 points

Spelling Test

Name   (3 pts.)

1. here
2. from
3. brim
4. have
5. drum
6. skid
7. there
8. smug
9. crop
10. grin

11. prop
12. smog
13. does *
14. are *   (20 pts.)
15. trot
16. scan
17. were
18. prim
19. brag
20. drop

The * denotes review words.

21. Where did he grab the scab on your skin?   (11 pts.)
22. She will be a crab and fret on the trip.   (12 pts.)

13

Lesson 5 – Initial Blend CCVC and CCCVC Words

> **Pattern-CCVC and CCCVC words:** snap snug span spin step stem swam swim quit quiz twig twin school scrap scrub shrug shrub split spry sprig squad squid strap strip throb

DIRECTIONS:

Review: Words from lessons 1, 2, 3, and 4.

New Words: This lesson is the last group of words stressing initial consonant blends. These CCVC words start with 14 different blends: sn - sp - st - sw - qu - tw - sch - scr - shr - spl - spr - squ - str - thr. Introduce each word in the spelling box and explain how to spell it by stressing the initial blend and the vowel sound. Explain the meaning of each word.

Show the students how to mark above the short vowel sound with a breve.

Dictate many of the extra words below and have students orally spell the words.

EXTRA WORDS:

snag snip snob spat spot sped stag stop stub stab swag
swig quip twit schoolbag scram shred splat strut

DICTATION SENTENCES:

I said do not snap the twig off of the shrub.
Have you quit swim school?
The twin squid swam by the crab.
The bug was snug on the stem.
When did I split a strip off my schoolbag strap?

TEST 5: 39 points

Spelling Test		Name	(3 pts.)
1. stem	11. prop		
2. shrug	12. smog		
3. snap	13. does *		
4. squad	14. are *		(20 pts.)
5. step	15. trot		
6. strip	16. scan		
7. sprig	17. were		
8. spin	18. prim		
9. squid	19. brag		
10. swam	20. drop		

The * denotes review words.

21. The bug was snug on the twig.   (9 pts.)
22. Have you quit swim school?   (7 pts.)

Lesson 6 – Final Blend CVCC and CCVCC Words

> **Pattern-CVCC and CCVCC words:** held cold told self shelf gulf milk calm psalm island grand fond fast must wrist brush flash squish bath with cloth   <u>Sight words</u>: been any many

DIRECTIONS:

Review: Words from lessons 1, 2, 3, 4, and 5.

New Words: This lesson is the first group of words stressing final consonant blends. These CVCC and CCVCC words end with 8 different blends: ld - lf - lk - lm - nd - st - sh - th. There are 3 new sight words. Introduce each word in the spelling box and explain how to spell it by stressing the initial blend, final blend, and the vowel sound. <u>Do not forget the silent 's' in island and the silent 'p' in psalm.</u> Explain the meaning of each word.

Show the students how to mark above the short vowel sound with a **breve** (ĕ). Show them how to mark above the long vowel sound with a **macron** (ē). A macron is short straight line like a subtract sign. **<u>Cold, told, and island</u>** have a long vowel.

Dictate many of the extra words below and have students orally spell the words.

EXTRA WORDS:

weld meld bold gold hold mold sold fold scold sand pond fund band brand dust mist twist blast past list fist blush dish fish rush mush flush path math broth moth elf golf bulk bilk sulk silk elk hulk palm overwhelm realm

DICTATION SENTENCES:

He told me many psalms.
Do I <u>take</u> a bath in the calm island gulf?
I held my brush with my wrists.
She did not have any grand cloth.
The milk on the shelf must not be cold.
The fish will twist in the pond.
The bold elf will rush past the sand on the path.
The list told me when I sold the gold dish.

TEST 6: 46 points

Spelling Test		Name	(3 pts.)
1. psalm	11. told		
2. where *	12. with		
3. brush	13. held		
4. many	14. flash		(20 pts.)
5. fast	15. any		
6. cloth	16. wrist		
7. squish	17. goes *		
8. been	18. fond		
9. grand	19. because *		
10. self	20. your *		

The * denotes review words.

21. The milk on the shelf must not be cold.   (11 pts.)
22. Do I <u>take</u> a bath in the calm island gulf?   (12 pts.)

Lesson 7 – Review Words

> The student's full name _ ? _ The teacher's name _ ? _ spelling test jam set sit got
> hum cab met win box bug has pen pin log nut chop chin shed shut that
> them when whip blot blab clap club flag flip glad glob plan plus sled slim
> brim brag crab crop drum drop fret from grin grab prop prim trip trot scab
> scan skid skin smog smug snap snug span spin step stem swam swim quit quiz
> twig twin school scrap scrub shrug shrub split spry sprig squad squid strap strip
> throb held told self shelf milk calm psalm island grand must wrist brush flash
> with cloth **said was they are of off because you your says goes does where**
> **were have there here been many any**

DIRECTIONS: This lesson is a review of short CVC words, words with initial blends, words with final blends, and sight words. There are 117 words, the student's complete name, and the teacher's name. Review all of the words in the Word Box by dictation.

EXTRA WORDS: Nothing this week

DICTATION SENTENCES: Nothing this week

TEST 7 REVIEW: 43 points

	Spelling Test		Name	(3 pts.)

1. chop
2. hum
3. brush
4. that
5. flip
6. many
7. cloth
8. been
9. grab
10. self

11. milk
12. they
13. squad
14. must
15. where
16. has
17. pen
18. sit
19. island
20. have

On the back side, have the students number their paper 21 through 40 along the side and the fold.

21. says
22. strap
23. jam
24. met
25. school
26. scrub
27. glad
28. trot
29. does
30. when

31. brag
32. whip
33. The teacher's name
34. quiz
35. because
36. calm
37. were
38. skin
39. flash
40. any   (40 pts.)

16

Lesson 8 – Final Blend CVCC and CCVCC Words

> **Pattern-CVCC and CCVCC words:** gulp scalp yelp felt melt wilt brisk
> desk mask bump stomp grasp crisp fact exact lift swift plant went
> print slept kept   <u>Sight words:</u> what want who

DIRECTIONS:

Review: Continually review the words from lessons 1, 2, 3, 4, 5, and 6.

New Words: This lesson is another group of words stressing final consonant blends. These CVCC and CCVCC words end with 9 different blends: lp - lt - sk - mp - sp - ct - ft - nt - pt. There are 3 new sight words. Introduce each word in the spelling box and explain how to spell it by stressing the initial blend, final blend, and the vowel sound. Explain the meaning of each word.

Show the students how to mark above the short vowel sound with a **breve**.

Dictate many of the extra words below and have students orally spell the words.

EXTRA WORDS:

help pulp belt pelt hilt jilt quilt jolt ask dusk flask frisk camp clamp damp slump limp ramp tramp jump stamp gasp clasp lisp wisp act pact tact tract craft draft drift loft raft theft soft bunt hunt hint lint sent grunt grant slant spent splint squint crept wept script rapt

DICTATION SENTENCES:

I gulp<u>ed</u> and yelp<u>ed</u> when I got a bump on my scalp!
I felt a bump on the desk.
Who will want a plant mask?
She kept the exact print of the facts in her desk.
The <u>cheese</u> will melt and the crisp <u>lettuce</u> will wilt.
The tramp crept into the damp camp and slept.
There was a hint of soft lint on the plant I sent to you.

TEST 8: 45 points

Spelling Test		Name	(3 pts.)

1. stomp
2. what
3. brisk
4. grasp
5. print
6. wilt
7. who
8. gulp
9. crisp
10. slept

11. exact
12. scalp
13. mask
14. kept   (20 pts.)
15. yelp
16. felt
17. bump
18. desk
19. melt
20. fact

21. I want to swift<u>ly</u> lift the plant off your desk.   (11 pts.)
22. He slept with a mask up on his scalp.   (11 pts.)

Lesson 9 – Final Blends <u>ng</u>, <u>nk</u>

> **Pattern-final blend "ng" words**: bang hang rang bring spring song strong belong lung stung   **Pattern-final blend "nk" words**: bank drank think wink shrink honk conk dunk skunk spunk   <u>Sight words</u>: only very really ever our

DIRECTIONS:

Review: Any of the words from the previous spelling boxes.

New Words: This lesson is the last group of words stressing final consonant blends. These CVCC and CCVCC words end with 2 different blends: ng and nk. There are 5 new sight words. Introduce each word in the spelling box and explain how to spell it by stressing the initial blend, final blend, and the vowel sound. Explain the meaning of each word.

DO NOT HAVE THE STUDENTS MARK THE VOWELS.

Dictate many of the extra words below and have students orally spell the words.

EXTRA WORDS:

fang sang clang sprang sing wing fling sling swing thing long bong gong prong throng hung sung flung swung strung sprung rank sank clank crank drank plank thank sink rink wink drink link slink sunk hunk drunk stunk shrunk

DICTATION SENTENCES:

She really has a lot of spunk.
The skunk sang a song by the bank of the spring.
You will need very strong lungs to sing that song.
They really belong at our bank.
Did you ever drink my pink drink all by yourself?
The bee stung me on my wrist as the <u>bell</u> rang.
Are you only winking?
Can you really swing on the thing in the rink?

TEST 9: 49 points

	Spelling Test		Name	(3 pts.)
1. drank		11. song		
2. ever		12. bang		
3. lung		13. skunk		
4. strong		14. conk		(20 pts.)
5. only		15. hang		
6. spring		16. bring		
7. wink		17. dunk		
8. spunk		18. shrink		
9. honk		19. think		
10. there *		20. many *		

The * denotes review words.

21. The pen really belongs at our bank.   (9 pts.)
22. She said the very mad bee stung her on the wrist as the <u>bell</u> rang.   (17 pts.)

Lesson 10 – Final Endings ff, ll, ss, zz

> **Pattern-endings ff, ll, ss, zz words:** bluff cliff puff sniff stuff buzz fuzz bell cell sell small smell thrill well yell bless class cross dress glass grass miss pass   <u>Sight words:</u> shall pull full

DIRECTIONS:

Review: Any of the words from the previous spelling boxes.

New Words: This lesson stresses group of words ending in ff, ll, ss, and zz. There are 3 new sight words that end with ll, but they have unusual vowel sounds. Introduce each word in the spelling box and explain how to spell it by stressing the initial blend, the double consonants at the end, and the vowel sound. Explain the meaning of each word.

Show the students how to mark above the short vowel sound with a **breve**.

Dictate many of the extra words below and have students orally spell the words.

EXTRA WORDS:

buff cuff fluff gruff huff muff scoff scuff staff stiff whiff ball bill bull chill doll drill dull fall fell fill frill gill grill gull hall hell hill hull ill lull mill pill quill roll* shell sill skill skull spill stall still stroll* swell tell till wall will bass bliss boss chess floss gloss hiss lass less loss mass mess moss press stress toss
*long vowel sounds

DICTATION SENTENCES:

The cells on the glass had a bad smell.
Did you miss the buzz of the class bell?
We will not roll on the grass by the cliff.
Shall we yell, hum, and pass bugs in here?
He will toss a very small fish on the grill.
Will you sell the small cross?
Where will we pass by the moss on the bluff?
Many <u>boys</u> will stroll down the hall with our balls.
Your scalp goes <u>over</u> your skull.

TEST 10: 45 points

Spelling Test		Name	(3 pts.)
1. sell	11. bell		
2. miss	12. pull		
3. stuff	13. bless		
4. sniff	14. bluff		(20 pts.)
5. grass	15. well		
6. class	16. fuzz		
7. thrill	17. cliff		
8. yell	18. pass		
9. puff	19. full		
10. shall	20. buzz		

21. I want the small cross for my school dress.   (10 pts.)
22. I think the cells on the glass had a bad smell.   (12 pts.)

Lesson 11- Number Words (one through ten)

Pattern-Number words: one two three four five six seven eight nine ten
<u>Sight words</u>: could should would won to too again against once
minute hour some something come over

DIRECTIONS:

Review: Any of the words from the previous spelling boxes.

New Words: The lesson consists of number words one to ten and several sight words. **This lesson will be harder for the students to memorize because the words do not belong to family groups and there are more sight words.** The students should take care to study these words more at home. Introduce each word in the spelling box and explain how to spell it by stressing any blend and the vowel sound. Explain the meaning of each word.

Stress the difference between the **homophones** (to, two, too) and (one, won).

DICTATION SENTENCES:

The seven flags flew over the island.
He could drink some milk, but should he?
They kept the four plants over against something.
Would you tell me the exact hour and minute you fell?
Did I pull one, two, or three bugs off the twig?
Eight quit, but one won the grand prize!
Do you ever want five pet skunks, too?
We did nine spins again and again.
Can you come over and swim in the gulf for one hour?

TEST 11: **48 points**

Spelling Test   Name   (3 pts.)

1. against
2. ten
3. could
4. something
5. one
6. too
7. once
8. over
9. eight
10. five

11. should
12. two
13. won
14. to   (20 pts.)
15. six
16. three
17. seven
18. come
19. four
20. minute

21. They did nine spins again and again for (the teacher's name).   (12 pts.)
22. Would you tell me the exact hour and minute you fell?   (13 pts.)

Lesson 12 – Beginning Sound <u>a</u> Words, <u>al</u> Words, <u>wa</u> Words

Pattern-"al" words: talk   walk   chalk   halt
Pattern-"wa" words: wash   water   watch   war   ward   warm
Pattern-beginning sound "a" words: about   alike   alive   along   away   above
across   awhile   ahead   asleep   amaze   afraid   around

DIRECTIONS: Review: Any of the words from the previous spelling boxes.

New Words: This lesson covers 23 "al" words, "wa" words, and words beginning with "a". There will not be any new sight words. Introduce each word in the spelling box and explain how to spell it by stressing any blend and the vowel sound. Explain the meaning of each word.

EXTRA WORDS:

stalk walnut wallet walrus wand waddle wander waffle wasp warden wart wardrobe award reward afar among ashore aware aboard abound

DICTATION SENTENCES:

I <u>am</u> not afraid to wash in warm water.
Do you ever like to talk about war?
We should walk across the park.
You may go ahead and sleep above in the loft.
Step around the glass and walk away with me.
The dog can wander around aboard the ship.
The man lost his wallet and will give you a reward if you <u>find</u> it.
The men will halt as they march about on the grass.
The ducks and the walrus will waddle ashore.
I talk very fast once in awhile.
If you watch her, she will amaze you.
(The teacher's name) cannot <u>find</u> any chalk.

TEST 12: 44 points

Spelling Test		Name	(3 pts.)
1. amaze		11. alive	
2. halt		12. could *	
3. awhile		13. won *	
4. ward		14. above	(20 pts.)
5. chalk		15. again *	
6. watch		16. minute *	
7. across		17. alike	
8. asleep		18. about	
9. talk		19. away	
10. war		20. ahead	

The * denotes review words.

21. I am not afraid to wash in warm water.   (10 pts.)
22. Step around the grass and walk along with me.   (11 pts.)

21

Lesson 13 – Review Sight Words and New Sight Words

<u>Review sight words:</u> could   should   would   won   again   against   once   hour   minute   to   too   shall   pull   full   what   who   want   said   was   they   are   of   off   because   you   your   says   over   come   some   something   only   very   really   ever   our   goes   does   where   were   have   there   here   been   many   any   <u>New sight words:</u>   use   no   know   much   such

DIRECTIONS:

Review: Any of the words from the previous spelling boxes.

New Words: This lesson reviews all 45 sight words of the previous 12 lessons. There are 5 new sight words. Introduce each word in the spelling box and explain how to spell it by stressing any blend and the vowel sound. Explain the meaning of each word. Stress the difference between the **homophones**.

DICTATION SENTENCES:

They were very afraid and ran off somewhere.
She says we want two full minutes to do our skit.
You shall pull the car over and then come here.
He was once very fast because he used his legs.
What do you have there in your hand?
No, we know we would have won only one <u>race</u>.
Have any of you ever been to the club much?
She does have such fun, so will you come again?
Who said you could come too?
Should she really run against him in the hour-long <u>race</u>?

TEST 13: 45 points

Spelling Test		Name	(3 pts.)
1. much	11. use		
2. minute	12. shall		
3. was	13. really		
4. because	14. very		(20 pts.)
5. where	15. been		
6. pull	16. many		
7. our	17. hour		
8. they	18. are		
9. does	19. again		
10. what	20. were		

21. No, we know we would have won only once against them.   (14 pts.)
22. Who said you could come too?   (8 pts.)

Lesson 14 – Money Words and "o" says short /ŭ/

> **Pattern-o says /ŭ/:** other mother another brother smother nothing month money
> **Pattern-Money words:** dollar quarter dime nickel penny pennies
> <u>Sight words</u>: else every pretty girl boy sister father people children

DIRECTIONS:

Review: Any of the words from the previous spelling boxes.

New Words: This lesson consists of money words and stresses "o say /ŭ/" words. There are 9 new sight words. Introduce each word in the spelling box and explain how to spell it by stressing any blend and the vowel sound. Explain the meaning of each word.

EXTRA WORDS: (Be sure to go over these words.)

done none oven love dove glove shove front ton son wonder dozen wagon

DICTATION SENTENCES:

Every father and mother wants some money.
People smother plants with water.
The boy and girl are very pretty twins.
May I have the other penny?
I got six dollars and eight quarters this month!
I <u>asked</u> where you got the five dimes and three nickels.
The girl and her other sister won ten dollars again.
The children want nothing but love.
The boy will shove the wagon.
The mother put a <u>pizza</u> in the oven.
Our brother has something else besides pennies!
I wonder where my glove is?

TEST 14: 53 points

Spelling Test		Name	(3 pts.)
1. people	11. penny		
2. sister	12. money		
3. else	13. quarter		
4. other	14. month	(20 pts.)
5. nothing	15. every		
6. nickel	16. children		
7. minute *	17. really *		
8. smother	18. brother		
9. dollar	19. pretty		
10. know *	20. another		

The * denotes review words.

21. The boys and girls get many dollars, quarters, dimes, nickels, and pennies every month. (20 pts.)

22. The father and mother have very pretty children. (10 pts.)

Lesson 15 – Review Words

scalp felt desk stomp crisp exact swift went kept slept hang sprang bring
strong belong lung bank think honk shrink skunk cliff buzz cell sell yell dress
bless grass smell one two three four five six seven eight chalk talk walk wash
water watch warm about alive alike along away above across awhile ahead
asleep amaze afraid around dollar quarter dime nickel penny pennies other
mother another brother smother nothing month money **they many any**
because says where were been are father people children sister every pretty
girl boy could should would won again against once hour minute to too shall
else use no know much such pull full what who want over come some
something only very really ever our

DIRECTIONS:

This lesson is a review of lessons 8 through 14. There are words with final blends, words ending in double consonants, number words, money words, "al", "wa", "a...", "o says /ŭ/ words, and many sight words. There are 120 words altogether. Review all the words in the Word Box by dictation.

EXTRA WORDS: Nothing this week

DICTATION SENTENCES: Nothing this week

TEST 15 Review: **43 points**

Spelling Test   Name   (3 pts.)

1. pretty
2. exact
3. pennies
4. warm
5. money
6. watch
7. quarter
8. belong
9. only
10. know

11. slept
12. children
13. again
14. seven
15. along
16. buzz
17. really
18. sell
19. around
20. mother

On the back side, have the students number their paper 21 through 40 along the side and the fold.

21. want
22. stomp
23. dollar
24. eight
25. bring
26. swift
27. would
28. once
29. minute
30. shrink

31. nickel
32. brother
33. above
34. people
35. ahead
36. our
37. many
38. were
39. been
40. afraid   (40 pts.)

Lesson 16 – Two Syllable Words

> **Pattern-Two syllable words:** pencil visit sudden sunset contest dentist selfish cabin magnet basket pony lazy tiny icy crazy truly lady baby zero
> **Sight words:** color Jesus Christ sure enough

DIRECTIONS:

Review: Any of the words from the previous spelling boxes.

New Words: This lesson consists of words made of two syllables. There are also five sight words. Introduce each word in the spelling box and explain how to spell it by stressing the syllables and the vowel sound. Explain the meaning of each word.

A syllable is a part of a word with a vowel in it. Every word is made of one or more syllables.

Closed syllables end with a consonant and have a short vowel sound. căb/ĭn vĭs/ĭt

Open syllables end with a vowel and have a long vowel sound. pō/ny(ē) zē/rō

Show the students how to divide the syllables and mark the vowel with breves and macrons.

EXTRA WORDS: (Be sure to go over these words.)

flatten habit invent napkin muffin holy navy
museum hero bony stony rabbit paper duty

DICTATION SENTENCES:

The crazy lady has a truly lazy pony.
As a habit, I flatten my napkin.
The dentist made a sudden visit to the cabin.
The bony hero was on duty at the museum.
Zero degrees is too icy for a tiny baby.
The stony magnet was not invented by the navy.
The selfish man could not see enough color in the sunset.
Jesus Christ helps me not to be selfish.
I am sure to win a pencil in the basket contest.
Our dentist loves Jesus Christ.

TEST 16: 47 points

Spelling Test	Name	(3 pts.)
1. enough	11. basket	
2. pencil	12. dentist	
3. sure	13. selfish	
4. visit	14. magnet	(20 pts.)
5. color	15. cabin	
6. sudden	16. icy	
7. really *	17. want *	
8. sunset	18. zero	
9. contest	19. any *	
10. hour *	20. pretty *	

The * denotes review words.

21. Jesus Christ was truly a tiny baby a long time ago. (14 pts.)
22. The crazy lady has a truly lazy pony. (10 pts.)

Lesson 17 – Vowel-consonant-e

Pattern-Vowel-consonant-e words: plane ate locate mistake pancake same hope before sunshine cube dislike beside escape invite admire cone pavement nicely decide write state   <u>Sight words:</u> friend sugar their

DIRECTIONS:

Review: Any of the words from the previous spelling boxes.

New Words: This lesson consists of words with <u>vowel - consonant - e</u> syllables. There are three sight words. Introduce each word in the spelling box and explain how to spell it by stressing the syllables and the vowel sound. Show how the <u>e</u> jumps over the consonant and makes the vowel sound long. Explain the meaning of each word.

A syllable is a part of a word with a vowel in it. Every word is made of one or more syllables.
<u>VCe syllables</u> end with the "e" vowel and make the vowel before it long.   brōke, dē/cīde
Show the students how to divide the syllables and mark the vowel with breves and macrons.

EXTRA WORDS: (There are many vowel-consonant-e words to chose).

cane page age sage hate rate plate late mate take bake lake made wade shade space wave tame shame came basement extreme sincere complete compete nice fine line dine pine mine mile file drive time pipe strife like rode doze robe broke drove rope stove ignore rule prune tune tube flute cute mule fume style type rhyme

DICTATION SENTENCES:

The girl will write nicely about their state on the notepad.
Did you want to eat the same sugar cone?
My brother ate their sugar cone on the plane by mistake.
She cannot decide if she should admire or dislike the sunshine.
I will nicely write on the pavement to invite my friends to eat pancakes.
My mother surely hopes to escape before we locate him.
I will ignore the slope of the basement.
She will take the plate of pancakes to that fine umpire.
Do you admire his friends?
He hopes we will have sunshine before you decide to invite his brother.

TEST 17: 48 points

	Spelling Test		Name	(3 pts.)
1.	escape	11.	enough *	
2.	ate	12.	state	
3.	plane	13.	write	
4.	sugar	14.	before	(20 pts.)
5.	nicely	15.	locate	
6.	invite	16.	cube	
7.	pavement	17.	pancake	
8.	mistake	18.	hope	
9.	color	19.	beside	
10.	their	20.	same	

The * denotes review word.

21. Father cannot decide if he should admire or dislike the sunshine.   (14 pts.)
22. Did your friends want to eat their sugar cones?   (11 pts.)

Lesson 18 – Diphthong i̲, y̲ says /ī/

> **Pattern-"igh" words**: lightning mightily mightier brightly high higher frightened nighttime **Pattern-" y̲" words**: flying dryer why reply **Pattern-"ie" words**: pie lie chief niece piece belief thief believe
> Sight words: laughed president almost own

DIRECTIONS:

Review: Any of the words from the previous spelling boxes.

New Words: This lesson consists of "i" diphthong words and y̲ says /ī / words. There are 4 new sight words. Introduce each word in the spelling box and explain how to spell it by stressing the syllables, the vowel sounds, and the suffixes. Be sure to point out the root words. Rehearse the sound rules over and over again. Explain the meaning of each word.

A syllable is a part of a word with a vowel in it. Every word is made of one or more syllables. Diphthongs are usually two vowel sounds joined in one syllable to form one speech sound. Sound rules: ig̲h̲ says /ī/ as in sight.   ie says /ē / as in thief   ie says /ī / as in pie
y̲ says /ī/ at the end of a syllable or word as in sky.
Show the students how to divide the syllables and mark the vowel with breves and macrons.

EXTRA WORDS:

light sight might night fight right fright bright mighty rightly frighten fighter sighted lighter sigh highest brief tie die my by dry cry shy sky deny crying

DICTATION SENTENCES:

Why did you reply that the chief is mightier than the President?
I almost had my own dryer.
He will die by nighttime.
It is my belief that my niece is a nighttime thief.
The light is so bright I could cry.
I believe I am flying higher, so do not get frightened.
He laughed mightily at the bright lightning in the sky.
The boy cannot deny his brief fight.
Why did you lie about the piece of pie?
Why does the President hate flying high in the lightning?

TEST 18: 43 points

| Spelling Test | Name | (3 pts.) |

1. reply
2. own
3. believe
4. pie
5. chief
6. nighttime
7. mightier
8. frightened
9. belief
10. lie

11. laughed
12. brightly
13. piece
14. higher
15. mightily
16. niece
17. president
18. thief
19. sugar *
20. their *

(20 pts.)

The * denotes review words.
21. Why does the President hate flying high in the lightning?   (13 pts.)
22. I almost had my own dryer.   (7 pts.)

Lesson 19 – Diphthong <u>a</u>

<u>**Pattern-"ai" words**</u>: sailor rain fail mailman sprain wait daily
<u>**Pattern-"ay" words**</u>: praying clay stay payment played
<u>**Pattern-"eigh" words**</u>: neighbor weight weigh
<u>**Pattern-"ey" words**</u>: obey survey hey
<u>Sight words</u>: these those through during gone none

DIRECTIONS:

Review: Any of the words from the previous spelling boxes.

New Words: This lesson consists of "a" diphthong words. There are 6 new sight words. Introduce each word in the spelling box and explain how to spell it by stressing the syllables, the vowel sounds, and the suffixes. Be sure to point out the root words. Rehearse the sound rules over and over again. Explain the meaning of each word.

A syllable is a part of a word with a vowel in it. Every word is made of one or more syllables. Diphthongs are usually two vowel sounds joined in one syllable to form one speech sound. Sound rules: <u>eigh</u> says /ā/ as in eight   <u>ai</u> says /ā/ as in rain   <u>ay</u> says /ā/ as in pray

<u>ey</u> says /ā/ at the end of a syllable or word as in they

Show the students how to divide the syllables and mark the vowel with breves and macrons.

EXTRA WORDS:

sail raining maid maiden trail rail mail waist gain pain paid slain train main
pray may play gay gray say hay pay day tray lay eight freight sleigh they grey

DICTATION SENTENCES:

A freight of hay came through the rain on the hay sleigh.
It will rain daily on the sailor during his wait.
I did a survey and one of those children played outside.
Father will weigh the clay before we play with it.
The maid will bring the light tray to you every day.
The mailman will obey and stay off his sprained <u>ankle</u>.
These boys and girls can obey as they wait to play!
Mother is praying our neighbor will not fail to make his payment.
Hey, my weight has gone down!

TEST 19: 49 points

Spelling Test	Name	(3 pts.)
1. pray	11. laughed *	
2. stay	12. brightly *	
3. weigh	13. weight	
4. those	14. played	(20 pts.)
5. obey	15. none	
6. sprain	16. mailman	
7. there *	17. survey	
8. their *	18. these	
9. hey	19. gone	
10. through	20. clay	

The * denotes review words.

21. Mother is praying our neighbor will not fail to make his payment.   (14 pts.)
22. It will rain daily on the sailor during his wait.   (12 pts.)

Lesson 20 – Diphthong e

> **Pattern-"ea" words**: tease weak feat steal sea leaf leaves plead meat seam
> **Pattern-"ee" words**: week feet steel see seem sweet meet speech freedom
> <u>Sight words</u>: sweat bread dead read head

DIRECTIONS:

Review: Any of the words from the previous spelling boxes.

New Words: This lesson consists of "e" diphthong words. There are 5 new sight words. Introduce each word in the spelling box and explain how to spell it by stressing the syllables, the vowel sounds, and the suffixes. Be sure to point out the root words. Rehearse the sound rules over and over again. Explain the meaning of each word.

A syllable is a part of a word with a vowel in it. Every word is made of one or more syllables.
Diphthongs are usually two vowel sounds joined in one syllable to form one speech sound.
Sound rules: <u>ee</u> says /ē/ as in bee   <u>ea</u> says /ē/ as in beach
Show the students how to divide the syllables and mark the vowel with breves and macrons.

EXTRA WORDS:

please eat beach team feast lead bead read reading reads eating seas pleaded defeated beaches weakness treat feed free need green tree speeches creed seed weed street teeming weedy seeing feeding sweetness needed meeting street

DICTATION SENTENCES:

People were meeting on the beaches to <u>hear</u> speeches over the weekend.
Our team ran through the leaves and weeds on the green beach.
I see the sea from the beach, and I will meet you there.
We need to feed the cat during the week, or he will get weak if he does not eat.
Before the play my sister put her feet through the seam of her leaf dress.
It seems there is a free feast of meat for you to eat.
Mother will plead with you not to tease the weak or steal from them.
The girl made a speech about freedom.
We ate the sweet bread while we were playing in the leaves.

TEST 20: 59 points

	Spelling Test		Name	(3 pts.)
1. feat		11. dead		
2. feet		12. read		
3. leaves		13. seam		
4. steel		14. leaf		(20 pts.)
5. speech		15. bread		
6. sweat		16. seem		
7. freedom		17. sea		
8. meat		18. sweet		
9. meet		19. hour *		
10. head		20. minute *		

The * denotes review words.

21. We need to feed the cat during the week, or he will get weak if he does not eat.   (21 pts.)
22. Jesus pleads with us not to tease the weak or steal from them.   (15 pts.)

Lesson 21 – Review Words

pencil visit sudden sunset contest dentist selfish cabin magnet basket pony lazy tiny icy crazy truly lady baby zero plane ate locate mistake pancake same hope before sunshine cube dislike beside escape invite admire cone pavement nicely decide write state lightning brightly mightily high mightier higher frightened nighttime flying dryer why reply chief niece piece belief thief believe pie lie sailor rain fail mailman sprain wait daily praying clay stay payment played neighbor weight weigh obey survey hey tease weak feat steal sea leaf leaves plead meat seam week feet steel see seem sweet meet speech freedom **sweat bread dead read head these those through during gone none laughed president almost own friend sugar their color Jesus Christ sure enough**

DIRECTIONS:

This lesson is a review of lessons 16 through 20. There are words with one or more syllables and many sight words. There are 120 words altogether. Review all the words in the Word Box by dictation.

EXTRA WORDS: Nothing this week

DICTATION SENTENCES: Nothing this week

TEST 21: 43 points

Spelling Test		Name	(3 pts.)
1. president		11. Jesus	
2. laughed		12. through	
3. sweat		13. neighbor	
4. mightier		14. escape	
5. crazy		15. sudden	
6. mistake		16. buzz	
7. sailor		17. believe	
8. reply		18. daily	
9. mailman		19. pavement	
10. pencil		20. decide	

On the back side, have the students number their paper 21 through 40 along the side and the fold.

21. almost		31. own	
22. sugar		32. friend	
23. basket		33. lightning	
24. chief		34. contest	
25. weigh		35. leaves	
26. speech		36. week	
27. obey		37. played	
28. sweet		38. steel	
29. piece		39. before	
30. color		40. Christ	(40 pts.)

30

Lesson 22 – Diphthong e, Diphthong o, y says /ē/

Pattern-"ei" words: receive ceiling	**Pattern-"ey" words**: monkey valley honey
Pattern-"oe" words: toe foe doe	
Pattern-"oa" words: boat road toast throat groan soap loaf loaves	
Pattern-"y" says /ē/ words: candy candies chilly sunny empty copy copies puppies	

DIRECTIONS:

Review: Any of the words from the previous spelling boxes.

New Words: This lesson consists of "e" diphthong words, "o" diphthong words, and y says /ē/ words. Introduce each word in the spelling box and explain how to spell it by stressing the syllables, the vowel sounds, and the suffixes. Be sure to point out the root words. Rehearse the sound rules over and over again. Explain the meaning of each word.

A syllable is a part of a word with a vowel in it. Every word is made of one or more syllables. Diphthongs are usually two vowel sounds joined in one syllable to form one speech sound.
Sound rules: ei says /ē/ as in receive   ey says /ē/ as in donkey
oe says /ō/ as in hoe   oa says /ō/ as in coat   y says /ē/ at the end of a word
"IE" rule: Use "i" before "e" except after "c", or when sounded like /ā/ as in neighbor and weigh.
Show the students how to divide the syllables and mark the vowel with breves and macrons.

EXTRA WORDS:

deceive conceit receipt key donkey turkey money chimney hoe woe toenail tiptoe coat coal float moat puppy mighty dusty rusty twenty thirty forty fifty sixty seventy eighty ninety silly filly baby sticky picky tricky

DICTATION SENTENCES:

She groaned in her throat when she hit her toe on the empty steel candy box.
Father received a monkey from the sunny valley.
You can use soap to get the sticky honey off the ceiling.
We rode on the road to get to the boat of cute puppies.
Noah put baby donkeys, monkeys, turkeys, and small does on the big dusty boat.
It was chilly in the valley so he started a fire under the chimney.
Mother made toast from the loaf of honey bread for my friends.
Her foe made copies of the many pages.

Test 22: 50 points

Spelling Test   Name   (3 pts.)

1. candies
2. doe
3. really *
4. valley
5. soap
6. loaves
7. where *
8. road
9. toe
10. monkey

11. receive
12. groan
13. sunny
14. copy   (20 pts.)
15. puppies
16. copies
17. boat
18. chilly
19. those *
20. ceiling

The * denotes review words.

21. My friend made toast from the loaf of honey bread.   (12 pts.)
22. His brother groaned in his throat when he received the empty candy box.   (15 pts.)

31

Lesson 23 – Diphthong <u>o</u>, Diphthong <u>u</u>, Soft <u>c</u> Words

Pattern-"ow" words: blow grow bowl slow	**Pattern-"eu" words**: Europe feud feudal
Pattern-"ew" words: few	**Pattern-"ue" words**: argue rescue
Pattern-"ie" words: view review	<u>Sight words</u>: door floor both easy
Pattern-Soft c words: face place mice fence since cents juice city	

DIRECTIONS:

Review: Any of the words from the previous spelling boxes.

New Words: This lesson consists of "o" diphthong words, "u" diphthong words, and words with the soft <u>c</u> sound. There are 4 sight words. Introduce each word in the spelling box and explain how to spell it by stressing the syllables, the vowel sounds, and the soft c sound. Rehearse the sound rules often. Explain the meaning of each word.

A syllable is a part of a word with a vowel in it. Every word is made of one or more syllables.
Diphthongs are usually two vowel sounds joined in one syllable to form one speech sound.
Sound rules: <u>ow</u> **says /ō/ as in snow** <u>ie</u> **says /yü/ as in view**
<u>ue</u> **says /yü/ as in rescue** <u>ew</u> **says /yü/ as in few** <u>eu</u> **says /yü/ as in feud**
"IE" rule: Use "i" before "e" except after "c", or when sounded like /ā/ as in neighbor and weigh.
The vowel sound in the "u" diphthong is marked: yü.
DO NOT HAVE THE STUDENTS MARK THE VOWELS.

EXTRA WORDS:

snow row mow low flow tow crow bow know cue pew new hew race lace trace ice price lice rice twice

DICTATION SENTENCES:

I think both books about mice are easy to read.
Please hand the bowl to me nice and easy.
The friends reviewed both pages since they were in view.
The feud will blow over when the boys grow up.
They paid a high price for that slow rescue at your place.
The children did not see a trace of snow from their pew.
I saw the faces of enough mice through the door.
Few men argued their place in feudal Europe.
My mother got a bowl of ice for the juice while she was in the city.

TEST 23: 49 points

	Spelling Test		Name	(3 pts.)

1. bowl
2. review
3. receive *
4. argue
5. Europe
6. mice
7. face
8. fence
9. slow
10. both

11. easy
12. few
13. place
14. view   (20 pts.)
15. city
16. floor
17. feudal
18. rescue
19. since
20. door

The * denotes review words.

21. The feud will blow over when the boys grow up   (12 pts.)
22. How many cents did you pay for the ice in your juice?   (14 pts.)

Lesson 24 – Diphthong <u>oo</u>

<u>Pattern-"ou" words</u>: soup group wound
<u>Pattern-"ue" words</u>: true glue due sue avenue
<u>Pattern-"oo" words</u>: food broom troop choose loose shoot soon tooth noon
<u>Pattern-"ew" words</u>: blew chew flew grew   <u>Sight words</u>: truth shoe sew

DIRECTIONS:

Review: Any of the words from the previous spelling boxes.

New Words: This lesson consists of "oo" diphthong words. There are 3 sight words.
Introduce each word in the spelling box and explain how to spell it by stressing the syllables and the vowel sounds. Rehearse the sound rules often. Explain the meaning of each word.
A syllable is a part of a word with a vowel in it. Every word is made of one or more syllables.
Diphthongs are usually two vowel sounds joined in one syllable to form one speech sound.
Sound rules: <u>ou</u> says /ü/ as in soup   <u>oo</u> says /ü/ as in noon
**   <u>ue</u> says /ü/ as in true   <u>ew</u> says /ü/ as in flew**
The vowel sound in the "oo" diphthong is marked: ü.
DO NOT HAVE THE STUDENTS MARK THE VOWELS.

EXTRA WORDS:

moon hoot droop cool room groom zoom blue clue tissue statue crew stew drew dew new toothpick toothbrush bathroom

DICTATION SENTENCES:

He blew on my toothbrush!
Is it true the troops have to shoot the brooms at noon?
Will mother sew or glue my shoe to fix it like new?
The group of children blew on the bowls of soup.
Jesus does not want us to sue others to gain money, and that is the truth.
I will choose right away to give you what is due to you.
The thief had a head wound <u>after</u> I hit him with a broom.
The boy grew up and flew his plane all over Europe.
An avenue is a street.

TEST 24: 54 points

	Spelling Test		Name	(3 pts.)
1.	wound	11.	loose	
2.	noon	12.	truth	
3.	sue	13.	broom	
4.	food	14.	soup	(20 pts.)
5.	due	15.	chew	
6.	juice *	16.	true	
7.	shoot	17.	flew	
8.	group	18.	choose	
9.	troop	19.	tooth	
10.	grew	20.	soon	

The * denotes review words.

21. Will my mother sew or glue my shoe to fix it like new?   (15 pts.)
22. His friend lives on Blew Street, not Blew Avenue.   (16 pts.)

33

Lesson 25 – Diphthong <u>oo</u>, Diphthong ô, Soft <u>c</u> Words

> **Pattern-"u" words**: push bushes   **Pattern-"au" words**: fault sauce cause pause author
> **Pattern-"oo" words**: stood wood took shook
> **Pattern-"aw" words**: jaw straw crawl awful   <u>Sight words</u>: hear give live busy
> **Pattern-Soft c words**: fancy center peace voice recess

DIRECTIONS:

Review: Any of the words from the previous spelling boxes.

New Words: This lesson consists of "oo" and "ô" diphthong words. There are five soft <u>c</u> words and 4 sight words. Introduce each word in the spelling box and explain how to spell it by stressing the syllables and the vowel sounds. Rehearse the sound rules often. Explain the meaning of each word.

A syllable is a part of a word with a vowel in it. Every word is made of one or more syllables. Diphthongs are usually two vowel sounds joined in one syllable to form one speech sound.
Sound rules: <u>u</u> says /oo/ as in put   <u>oo</u> says /oo/ as in book
DO NOT HAVE THE STUDENTS MARK THE VOWELS. u and oo are marked: /u with a small dot over the u/
<u>au</u> says /ô/ as in pause   <u>aw</u> says /ô/ as in law   au and aw are marked: /o with a small dot/

EXTRA WORDS:

put putting pull full butcher book look good hood cook foot ball softball hall talk small war faucet gauze haunt law paw claw dawn scrawl lawn flaw awesome

DICTATION SENTENCES:

The author wrote a book about making peace at recess time.
I read a book on the lawn.
She stood on the sod and saw me crawl through the bushes.
I crawled to get to the center of the straw pile.
I hope you know that cause and because are not the same.
Busy mother shook the fancy sauce before she took it off the stove.
It is your fault you got pushed when you paused in line at recess.
Please give my jaw a nice push with your foot!
My sister will give me a voice test to see if I am a good singer.
Did the President hear the awful news?

TEST 25: 52 points

Spelling Test   Name   (3 pts.)

1. push
2. hear
3. fancy
4. jaw
5. stood
6. give
7. center
8. straw
9. sauce
10. wood

11. live
12. voice
13. awful
14. took   (20 pts.)
15. author
16. busy
17. peace
18. crawl
19. shook
20. bushes

21. It was your fault you got pushed when you paused in line at recess.   (16 pts.)
22. Do you know that cause and because are not the same?   (13 pts.)

Lesson 26 – Diphthong <u>ou</u>, Hard <u>c</u> Words, Consonant <u>le</u> Syllable Words

Pattern-"ou" words: loud house shout mouth found ounce	**Pattern-Hard c words**:
Pattern-"ow" words: how growl downtown towel	climb castle country
Pattern-ble words: bubble marble stable tremble	comb cotton crocodile
Pattern-dle words: bundle candle puddle middle	

DIRECTIONS:

Review: Any of the words from the previous spelling boxes.

New Words: This lesson consists of "ou" diphthong words, hard <u>c</u> words, and <u>consonant-le</u> syllable words. Introduce each word in the spelling box and explain how to spell it by stressing the syllables and the vowel sounds. Rehearse the sound rules. Explain the meaning of each word. **A syllable is a part of a word with a vowel in it. Every word is made of one or more syllables. Diphthongs are usually two vowel sounds joined in one syllable to form one speech sound. Sound rules:** <u>ou</u> **says /ou/ as in out** <u>ow</u> **says /ou/ as in cow ou and ow are marked:** /au with a small dot above the u/ **DO NOT HAVE THE STUDENTS MARK THE VOWELS.**

EXTRA WORDS:

cracker crab cord cake county out our cloud mouse stout south round pound sound pounce ground cow now plow owl brown flower howl ramble table tumble thimble cradle idle

DICTATION SENTENCES:

How can we climb to the top of the marble castle?
The owl ate the cracker.
They found a bubble in the middle of the puddle.
The loud mouth will make me tremble when he shouts in the house.
The stable belongs in the country and not downtown.
The girl will bundle the candle up in the cotton towel.
His friend combed the country looking for a crocodile.
How many ounces are in a pound?
The stout chief had a mean growl.
The mouse will pounce on the brown cow.
I found her round thimble on the table.

TEST 26: 49 points

	Spelling Test	Name	(3 pts.)

1. tremble
2. ounce
3. crocodile
4. growl
5. marble
6. castle
7. shout
8. climb
9. bundle
10. piece *

11. towel
12. comb
13. house
14. mouth   (20 pts.)
15. candle
16. cotton
17. loud
18. how
19. peace *
20. their *

The * denotes review words.

21. Some people found a bubble in the middle of the puddle.   (13 pts.)
22. The stable and house belong in the country and not downtown.   (13 pts.)

Lesson 27 – Review Words

receive ceiling monkey valley honey toe foe doe boat road toast throat groan soap loaf loaves candy candies chilly sunny empty copy copies puppies blow grow bowl slow Europe feud feudal few argue rescue view review face place mice fence since cents juice city blew chew flew grew soup group wound true glue due sue avenue choose food broom troop loose shoot soon tooth noon push bushes fault sauce cause pause author stood wood took shook jaw straw crawl awful fancy center peace voice recess loud house shout mouth found ounce how growl downtown towel climb castle comb country cotton crocodile bubble marble stable tremble bundle candle puddle middle **live give hear busy truth shoe sew door floor both easy**

DIRECTIONS:

This lesson is a review of lessons 22 through 26. There are words with one or more syllables and many sight words. There are 120 words altogether. Review all of the words in the Word Box by dictation.

EXTRA WORDS: Nothing this week

DICTATION SENTENCES: Nothing this week

TEST 27: 43 points

Spelling Test	Name	(3 pts.)

1. truth
2. sew
3. floor
4. middle
5. tremble
6. growl
7. voice
8. recess
9. climb
10. bushes

11. castle
12. country
13. crocodile
14. ounce
15. awful
16. mouth
17. shook
18. avenue
19. author
20. choose

On the back side, have the students number their paper 21 through 40 along the side and the fold.

21. receive
22. toast
23. few
24. house
25. bowl
26. loaves
27. rescue
28. since
29. chew
30. group

31. valley
32. empty
33. feud
34. cents
35. soup
36. puppies
37. fence
38. place
39. review
40. juice   (40 pts.)

Lesson 28 – Diphthong <u>oi</u> and Consonant <u>le</u> Syllable Words

Pattern-"oi" words: soil coin join point poison	
Pattern-"oy" words: toy enjoy royal destroy	**Pattern-fle words**: rifle ruffle sniffle
Pattern-ple words: apple dimple sample	**Pattern-kle words**: ankle buckle tickle
Pattern-gle words: giggle jungle single struggle	sparkle twinkle

DIRECTIONS:

Review: Any of the words from the previous spelling boxes.

New Words: This lesson consists of "oi" diphthong words and more <u>consonant-le</u> syllable words. Introduce each word in the spelling box and explain how to spell it by stressing the syllables and the vowel sounds. Rehearse the sound rules often. Explain the meaning of each word.

A syllable is a part of a word with a vowel in it. Every word is made of one or more syllables. Diphthongs are usually two vowel sounds joined in one syllable to form one speech sound. Sound rules: <u>oi</u> **says /oi/ as in boil** <u>oy</u> **says /oi/ as in boy**
oi and oy are marked: /oi each having one small dot over them/
DO NOT HAVE THE STUDENTS MARK THE VOWELS.

EXTRA WORDS:

oil boil toil void moist boy joy coy soybean oyster baffle stifle
bugle smuggle gargle pickle ripple staple rumple topple trample

DICTATION SENTENCES:

He did not find a single monkey in the jungle.
Did you enjoy the sample of the green apple?
The pretty girl has a dimple on her chin and a sparkle in her *eye*.
My sister will twinkle her <u>eyes</u> when she sees the ruffle on her new dress.
The oil will make the cake very moist.
The toy rifle does not shoot a poison point!
We tickled his ankles <u>until</u> he got the giggles and the sniffles.
They will struggle to destroy the royal ship full of soiled coins.
We need to join the buckle on the belt.

TEST 28: 49 points

Spelling Test	Name	(3 pts.)

1. Jesus *
2. Christ *
3. tickle
4. apple
5. ruffle
6. join
7. twinkle
8. sniffle
9. point
10. ankle

11. pretty *
12. sparkle
13. toy
14. dimple (20 pts.)
15. enjoy
16. poison
17. sample
18. buckle
19. rifle
20. giggle

The * denotes review words.

21. He did not find a single monkey in the jungle. (12 pts.)
22. They will struggle to destroy the royal ship full of soiled coins! (14 pts.)

Lesson 29 – Diphthong <u>er</u> and Consonant <u>le</u> Syllable Words

Pattern-"er" words: jerk verse nerve perch stem winter upper answer
Pattern-"ir" words: bird thirst shirt chirp third
Pattern-tle words: battle bottle little settle   **Pattern-stle words**: wrestle hustle whistle
Pattern-zle words: puzzle fizzle   <u>Sight words</u>: woman women

DIRECTIONS:

Review: Any of the words from the previous spelling boxes.

New Words: This lesson consists of "er" diphthong words and more <u>consonant-le</u> syllable words. There are 2 new sight words. Introduce each word in the spelling box and explain how to spell it by stressing the syllables and the vowel sounds. Rehearse the sound rules often. Explain the meaning of each word.

A syllable is a part of a word with a vowel in it. Every word is made of one or more syllables. Diphthongs are usually two vowel sounds joined in one syllable to form one speech sound. Sound rules: <u>er</u> says /er/ as in her   <u>ir</u> says /er/ as in dirt
DO NOT HAVE THE STUDENTS MARK THE VOWELS.

EXTRA WORDS:

her fern term stir girl firm birth birthday dirt flirt squirt cattle
whittle shuttle dazzle sizzle drizzle frazzle thistle jostle nestle

DICTATION SENTENCES:

The little bird sat on his perch and <u>tried</u> to chirp.
The third verse is the right answer.
His nerve will fizzle when he goes to battle during the winter.
The woman likes to whistle while she does the puzzle.
Do not jerk on my shirt while I wrestle.
The first bottle will settle down on the upper shelf.
The stern women hustle through their work, and they do not play.
The little thistle will frazzle the women.
I like to whittle cattle and birds from a piece of wood.

TEST 29: 46 points

Spelling Test		Name	(3 pts.)
1. stern	11. little		
2. bird	12. first		
3. puzzle	13. upper		
4. perch	14. jerk		(20 pts.)
5. woman	15. bottle		
6. whistle	16. hustle		
7. really *	17. chirp		
8. laughed	18. should		
9. wrestle	19. women		
10. shirt	20. settle		

The * denotes review words.

21. The third verse is the right answer.   (9 pts.)
22. His nerve will fizzle when he goes to battle during the winter.   (14 pts.)

Lesson 30 – Diphthong er, Complete Address & Phone Number

Pattern-"ur" words: hurt burn nurse turn **Pattern-"ar" words**: beggar cellar dollar collar
Pattern-"or" words: worm work worship world word worth worse doctor
Pattern-"ear" words: earn learn search heard earth early   Sight words: whose pint
Know your complete address and complete phone number

DIRECTIONS:
Review: Any of the words from the previous spelling boxes.
New Words: This lesson consists of "er" diphthong words and 2 new sight words. The students will also need to know their complete address and complete phone number. Introduce each word in the spelling box and explain how to spell it by stressing the syllables and the vowel sounds. Rehearse the sound rules often. Explain the meaning of each word.
A syllable is a part of a word with a vowel in it. Every word is made of one or more syllables.
Diphthongs are usually two vowel sounds joined in one syllable to form one speech sound.
Sound rules: ur says /er/ as in fur   or says /er/ as in work   ear says /er/ as in earth
**   ar says /er/ as in dollar   DO NOT HAVE THE STUDENTS MARK THE VOWELS.**

EXTRA WORDS:
fur surf chum suburb lurk turf purr humor
pearl research calendar regular earthworms

DICTATION SENTENCES:
She took a turn for the worse.
It is worth your time to learn about the world.
The men and women heard the early worship bell.
The beggar was searching for earthworms so he could go fishing.
I need a doctor or a nurse to look at my burn that hurts.
The girl searched the cellar for the dollar she earned at work last week.
Whose collar was turned up?
I took a pint of earth from my cellar to school.
They heard a word of <u>thanksgiving</u> from the nurse and the doctor.

TEST 30: 73 points

Spelling Test   Name   (3 pts.)

1. whose	11. pint
2. collar	12. worse
3. worship	13. nurse
4. hurt	14. earn (20 pts.)
5. word	15. turn
6. doctor	16. dollar
7. would *	17. burn
8. poison *	18. sugar *
9. early	19. work
10. cellar	20. heard

The * denotes review words.

21. The beggar was up early to search for earthworms so he could go fishing.   (16 pts.)
22. It is worth your time to learn about the world.   (12 pts.)
First name   middle name   last name   (6 pts.)
Complete Address   (5 pts.)
City, State   Zip Code   (6 pts.)
(Area Code) Prefix Suffix   (5 pts.)

Lesson 31 – Days of the Week, Color Words, Address & Phone Number

> **Pattern-Days of the week**: Sunday Monday Tuesday Wednesday Thursday Friday
> Saturday   Sight words: which care pair pear tear wear bear
> **Pattern-Color words**: yellow orange red pink purple blue green brown black white
> **Know your complete address and complete telephone number**

DIRECTIONS:

Review: Any of the words from the previous spelling boxes.

New Words: This lesson covers the days of the weeks and color words. There are 7 new sight words. There is a review of the student's complete address and complete telephone number. Introduce each word in the spelling box and explain how to spell it by stressing the syllables and the vowel sounds. Make sure the students understand the meanings of the homophones.

A syllable is a part of a word with a vowel in it. Every word is made of one or more syllables.

EXTRA WORDS:

pare mare rare fare tare dare scare stare stair
fair hair haircut swear gray navy violet

DICTATION SENTENCES:

Which day of the week do you like best?
Sunday was a fair day.
My friend likes Wednesday best of all.
My <u>favorite</u> color is yellow.
The bear ate a pair of pears on Friday.
May I wear my brown and pink dress?
He said he liked Tuesday and Thursday the best because they start with T.
Please take good care of your purple and pink shirt.
The bear will tear the orange and eat it.
Father got his black hair cut on Monday.
Do you like my haircut?

TEST 31: 68 points

Spelling Test		Name	(3 pts.)
1. which	11. purple		
2. white	12. Tuesday		
3. Wednesday	13. care		
4. wear	14. yellow		(20 pts.)
5. pink	15. green		
6. Sunday	16. Friday		
7. orange	17. brown		
8. tear	18. blue		
9. red	19. Monday		
10. any *	20. children		

The * denotes review words.

21. Father had his black hair cut on Thursday.	(11 pts.)
22. Last Saturday the bear ate a pair of pears.	(12 pts.)
First name middle name last name	(6 pts.)
Complete Address	(5 pts.)
City, State Zip Code	(6 pts.)
(Area Code) Prefix Suffix	(5 pts.)

Lesson 32 – Months of the Year, Address & Phone Number

Pattern-Months of the year: January February March April May June July August September October November December
Know your complete address and complete phone number   <u>Sight words</u>: heaven hell devil Satan God lamb Bible Almighty Holy Spirit parents animals

DIRECTIONS:

Review: Any of the words from the previous spelling boxes.

New Words: This lesson covers the months of the year. There are 12 new sight words. There is a review of the student's complete address and complete telephone number. Introduce each word in the spelling box and explain how to spell it by stressing the syllables and the vowel sounds. **A syllable is a part of a word with a vowel in it. Every word is made of one or more syllables.**

EXTRA WORDS: None this week

DICTATION SENTENCES:

The spring months are March, April, and May.
The summer months are June, July, and August.
The fall months are September, October, and November.
The winter months are December, January, and February.
The Holy Spirit lives in people if they belong to Jesus Christ.
Do you like the months of November and December?
In heaven everyone will worship the Lord God Almighty and the Lamb.
Satan is another name for the devil.
I want my parents to live <u>forever</u> in heaven.
There will not be animals in hell.

TEST 32: 77 points

Spelling Test   Name   (3 pts.)

1. January	11. September	
2. February	12. October	
3. June	13. November	
4. July	14. December	(20 pts.)
5. Satan	15. August	
6. devil	16. heaven	
7. lamb	17. God	
8. tear *	18. Spirit	
9. Almighty	19. Bible	
10. parents	20. animals	

The * denotes review words.

21. The Holy Spirit lives in people if they belong to Jesus Christ.   (18 pts.)
22. The spring months are March, April, and May.   (14 pts.)
First name middle name last name   (6 pts.)
Complete Address   (5 pts.)
City, State Zip Code   (6 pts.)
(Area Code) Prefix Suffix   (5 pts.)

Lesson 33 – Review Words

soil coin join point poison toy enjoy royal destroy apple dimple sample giggle
jungle single struggle riffle ruffle sniffle ankle buckle tickle sparkle twinkle jerk
verse nerve perch stern winter upper answer bird thirst shirt chirp third battle
bottle little settle puzzle fizzle wrestle hustle whistle hurt burn nurse turn beggar
cellar dollar collar worm work worship world word worth worse doctor earn
learn search heard earth early Sunday Monday Tuesday Wednesday Thursday
Friday Saturday yellow orange red pink purple blue green brown black white
January February March April May June July August September October
November December **hell heaven devil Satan God lamb Bible Almighty Holy Spirit
animals parents which care pair pear tear wear bear whose pint woman women**

DIRECTIONS: This lesson is a review of lessons 28 through 32. There are words with one or more syllables and many sight words. There are 120 words altogether. Review all of the words in the Word Box by dictation. Make sure the students know the difference between the homophones.

EXTRA WORDS: Nothing this week

DICTATION SENTENCES: Nothing this week

TEST 33: 43 points

Spelling Test   Name   (3 pts.)

1. heaven
2. Satan
3. whose
4. which
5. August
6. January
7. purple
8. orange
9. Wednesday
10. Thursday

11. lamb
12. animals
13. pair
14. parents
15. women
16. December
17. February
18. Tuesday
19. Saturday
20. early

On the back side, have the students number their paper 21 through 40 along the side and the fold.

21. heard
22. worse
23. worship
24. dollar
25. wrestle
26. thirst
27. struggle
28. point
29. rifle
30. buckle

31. learn
32. doctor
33. burn
34. third
35. little
36. answer
37. verse
38. giggle
39. enjoy
40. sparkle   (40 pts.)

Lesson 34 – <u>tch</u>, <u>g</u>, <u>dge</u>, and <u>r-controlled</u> Words

> **Pattern-"g" words**: strange huge change
> **Pattern-"dge" words**: badge judge dodge budge pledge
> **Pattern-r-controlled words**: farm hard large heart force horse morning starfish popcorn airport   **Pattern-"tch" words**: ditch stretch sketch catch scratch crutch

DIRECTIONS:

Review: Any of the words from the previous spelling boxes.

New Words: This lesson consists of <u>tch</u> words, <u>g</u> words, <u>dge</u> words, and <u>r-controlled</u> words. Introduce each word in the spelling box and explain how to spell it by stressing the syllables and the vowel sounds. Explain the meaning of each word.

A syllable is a part of a word with a vowel in it. Every word is made of one or more syllables.

EXTRA WORDS:

match hatch snatch patch pitch stitch pitcher wage stage cage fudge car card star harm horn hornet fork pork cork corn storm form morn hair air haircut pair stair fair

DICTATION SENTENCES:

The farm horse stretched and dodged the large ditch.
The strange starfish would not budge.
The judge used his crutch at the airport.
He needs to scratch under the huge badge.
It takes much force to change popcorn.
Do you want to play dodge ball or catch the softball?
The hard judge took a pledge Monday morning.
I know in my heart I should force you to change the pledge.
My friend found the starfish in the ditch next to the airport.

TEST 34: 41 points total

Spelling Test		Name	(3 pts.)
1. ditch		11. stretch	
2. farm		12. hard	
3. sketch		13. dodge	
4. Wednesday *		14. airport	(20 pts.)
5. huge		15. August *	
6. catch		16. scratch	
7. horse		17. large	
8. pledge		18. morning	
9. judge		19. badge	
10. crutch		20. heart	

The * denotes review words.

21. The strange starfish would not budge.   (8 pts.)
22. It took much force to change the popcorn.   (10 pts.)

Lesson 35 – Number Words (eleven through twenty) and Contractions

Pattern-Number words: eleven twelve thirteen fourteen fifteen sixteen seventeen eighteen nineteen twenty **Pattern-Contractions**: you're they're we're doesn't didn't won't that's he's I've you'll she'll Sight words: fought bought thought

DIRECTIONS:

Review: Any of the words from the previous spelling boxes.

New Words: This lesson consists of number words and contractions. There are 3 sight words. Introduce each word in the spelling box and explain how to spell it by stressing the syllables and the vowel sounds. Explain the meaning of each word.

Show the students how two words make a contraction.

A syllable is a part of a word with a vowel in it. Every word is made of one or more syllables.

EXTRA WORDS:

aren't hasn't wasn't haven't hadn't weren't don't can't isn't we'll he'll they'll what's let's who's there's I'd I'm I'll you're they've we've couldn't wouldn't shouldn't

DICTATION SENTENCES:

I thought sixteen or seventeen drinks of water were too much.
Your fourteen horses jumped the ditch.
They're running to dodge the ball.
I've done the work, and I'm ready to go home now.
Doesn't he want to eat twenty eggs?
The knight fought thirteen battles for the castle.
You're going to play eleven games today.
You'll see fifteen girls in the classroom.
That's the best thought you can have on your mind.
Didn't he grab the twelve softballs?
She'll cook nineteen pancakes this morning.
We're sitting at the store.
He's wearing a mask on his face.
People won't try the scary ride.
He bought eighteen toys today.

TEST 35: 48 points

Spelling Test   Name   (3 pts.)

1. eleven
2. fourteen
3. they're
4. seventeen
5. fifteen
6. I've
7. bought
8. sixteen
9. you'll
10. we're

11. fought
12. she'll
13. eighteen
14. doesn't   (20 pts.)
15. twenty
16. didn't
17. that's
18. nineteen
19. won't
20. he's

21. I thought twelve or thirteen pancakes were too much for you to eat.   (14 pts.)
22. You're going to do your homework right this minute!   (11 pts.)

Lesson 36 – Review Words

Sunday Monday Tuesday Wednesday Thursday Friday Saturday January February March April May June July August September October November December ditch stretch sketch catch scratch crutch strange huge change badge judge dodge budge pledge farm hard large heart force horse morning starfish popcorn airport eleven twelve thirteen fourteen fifteen sixteen seventeen eighteen nineteen twenty you're they're we're doesn't didn't won't that's he's I've you'll she'll **heaven hell devil Satan God lamb Bible Almighty Holy Spirit animals which pear tear wear bear whose pint woman women hear busy truth shoe sew care pair sweat bread head read dead these those through gone to door floor both easy live almost own friend sugar their father people during too none laughed president pretty girl boy else use no know much such children every color Jesus Christ sure fought bought thought parents could should would won again against once hour over come some something only very really ever our goes does where were have there here been many any give minute shall pull full what who want said was they enough are of off because you your says**

DIRECTIONS: This lesson is a review of the last three lessons and 119 sight words. There are 183 words altogether. Review all of the words in the Word Box by dictation. Make sure the students know the difference between the homophones.

DICTATION SENTENCES: Nothing this week

TEST 36: 43 points

Spelling Test   Name   (3 pts.)

1. children
2. president
3. strange
4. Tuesday
5. they're
6. heaven
7. where
8. again
9. Wednesday
10. scratch
11. truth
12. Saturday
13. sugar
14. any
15. bread
16. should
17. February
18. morning
19. eighteen
20. change

On the back side, have the students number their paper 21 through 40 along the side and the fold.

21. Thursday
22. twelve
23. pledge
24. August
25. doesn't
26. during
27. struggle
28. through
29. woman
30. twenty
31. fifteen
32. January
33. thought
34. really
35. enough
36. pretty
37. you're
38. thirteen
39. because
40. friend

(40 pts.)

BLANK PAGE

Master List of Spelling Words

(The student's full name) _____
(The teacher's name) _____
    Sight words: spelling test said was they are of off because

Lesson 1

Pattern-CVC words: jam set sit got hum cab net win box bug
has pen pin log nut   Sight words: spelling test said was because

Lesson 2

Pattern-CCVC words: chop chin shed shut that them when whip blot
blab clap club flag flip glad glob plan plus sled slim
Sight words: you your says goes does

Lesson 3

Pattern-CCVC words: brim brag crab crop drum drop fret from grin
grab prop prim trip trot scab scan skid skin smog smug
Sight words: where were have there here

Lesson 4

Pattern-CCVC and CCCVC words: snap snug span spin step stem swam
swim quit quiz twig twin school scrap scrub shrug shrub split spry
sprig squad squid strap strip throb

Lesson 5

Pattern-CVCC and CCVCC words: held cold told self shelf gulf milk calm
psalm island grand fond fast must wrist brush flash squish bath with
cloth   Sight words: been any many

Lesson 6

The student's full name _ ? _ The teacher's name _ ? _ spelling test jam set sit got
hum cab met win box bug has pen pin log nut chop chin shed shut that
them when whip blot blab clap club flag flip glad glob plan plus sled slim
brim brag crab crop drum drop fret from grin grab prop prim trip trot scab
scan skid skin smog smug snap snug span spin step stem swam swim quit quiz
twig twin school scrap scrub shrug shrub split spry sprig squad squid strap strip
throb held told self shelf milk calm psalm island grand must wrist brush flash
with cloth **said was they are of off because you your says goes does where
were have there here been many any**

Lesson 7- Review

Pattern-CVCC and CCVCC words: gulp scalp yelp felt melt wilt brisk desk mask bump stomp grasp crisp fact exact lift swift plant went print slept kept <u>Sight words:</u> what want who

Lesson 8

Pattern-final blend "ng" words: bang hang rang bring spring song strong belong lung stung **Pattern-final blend "nk" words:** bank drank think wink shrink honk conk dunk skunk spunk <u>Sight words:</u> only very really ever our

Lesson 9

Pattern-endings ff, ll, ss, zz words: bluff cliff puff sniff stuff buzz fuzz bell cell sell small smell thrill well yell bless class cross dress glass grass miss pass <u>Sight words:</u> shall pull full

Lesson 10

Pattern-Number words: one two three four five six seven eight nine ten <u>Sight words:</u> could should would won to too again against once minute hour some something come over

Lesson 11

Pattern-"al" words: talk walk chalk halt
Pattern-"wa" words: wash water watch war ward warm
Pattern-beginning sound "a" words: about alike alive along away above across awhile ahead asleep amaze afraid around

Lesson 12

<u>Review sight words:</u> could should would won again against once hour minute to too shall pull full what who want said was they are of off because you your says over come some something only very really ever our goes does where were have there here been many any <u>New sight words:</u> use no know much such

Lesson 13

Pattern-o says /ŭ/: other mother another brother smother nothing month money
Pattern-Money words: dollar quarter dime nickel penny pennies
<u>Sight words:</u> else every pretty girl boy sister father people children

Lesson 14

scalp felt desk stomp crisp exact swift went kept slept hang sprang bring strong belong lung bank think honk shrink skunk cliff buzz cell sell yell dress bless grass smell one two three four five six seven eight chalk talk walk wash water watch warm about alive alike along away above across awhile ahead asleep amaze afraid around dollar quarter dime nickel penny pennies other mother another brother smother nothing month money **they many any because says where were been are father people children sister every pretty girl boy could should would won again against once hour minute to too shall else use no know much such pull full what who want over come some something only very really ever our**

Lesson 15 - Review

Pattern-Two syllable words: pencil visit sudden sunset contest dentist selfish cabin magnet basket pony lazy tiny icy crazy truly lady baby zero
Sight words: color Jesus Christ sure enough

Lesson 16

Pattern-Vowel-consonant-e words: plane ate locate mistake pancake same hope before sunshine cube dislike beside escape invite admire cone pavement nicely decide write state   Sight words: friend sugar their

Lesson 17

Pattern-"igh" words: lightning mightily mightier brightly high higher frightened nighttime **Pattern-"y" words:** flying dryer why reply
Pattern-"ie" words: pie lie chief niece piece belief thief believe
Sight words: laughed president almost own

Lesson 18

Pattern-"ai" words: sailor rain fail mailman sprain wait daily
Pattern-"ay" words: praying clay stay payment played
Pattern-"eigh" words: neighbor weight weigh
Pattern-"ey" words: obey survey hey
Sight words: these those through during gone none

Lesson 19

Pattern-"ea" words: tease weak feat steal sea leaf leaves plead meat seam
Pattern-"ee" words: week feet steel see seem sweet meet speech freedom
Sight words: sweat bread dead read head

Lesson 20

49

pencil visit sudden sunset contest dentist selfish cabin magnet basket pony lazy
tiny icy crazy truly lady baby zero plane ate locate mistake pancake same
hope before sunshine cube dislike beside escape invite admire cone pavement
nicely decide write state lightning brightly mightily high mightier higher
frightened nighttime flying dryer why reply chief niece piece belief thief believe
pie lie sailor rain fail mailman sprain wait daily praying clay stay payment
played neighbor weight weigh obey survey hey tease weak feat steal sea leaf
leaves plead meat seam week feet steel see seem sweet meet speech
freedom **sweat bread dead read head these those through during gone none**
laughed president almost own friend sugar their color Jesus Christ sure enough

Lesson 21 - Review

Pattern-"ei" words: receive ceiling   **Pattern-"ey" words**: monkey valley honey
Pattern-"oe" words: toe foe doe
Pattern-"oa" words: boat road toast throat groan soap loaf loaves
Pattern-"y" says /ē/ words: candy candies chilly sunny empty copy copies puppies

Lesson 22

Pattern-"ow" words: blow grow bowl slow **Pattern-"eu" words**: Europe feud feudal
Pattern-"ew" words: few   **Pattern-"ue" words**: argue rescue
Pattern-"ie" words: view review   Sight words: door floor both easy
Pattern-Soft c words: face place mice fence since cents juice city

Lesson 23

Pattern-"ou" words: soup group wound
Pattern-"ue" words: true glue due sue avenue
Pattern-"oo" words: food broom troop choose loose shoot soon tooth noon
Pattern-"ew" words: blew chew flew grew   Sight words: truth shoe sew

Lesson 24

Pattern-"u" words: push bushes   **Pattern-"au" words**: fault sauce cause pause author
Pattern-"oo" words: stood wood took shook
Pattern-"aw" words: jaw straw crawl awful   Sight words: hear give live busy
                    Pattern-Soft c words: fancy center peace voice recess

Lesson 25

Pattern-"ou" words: loud house shout mouth found ounce   **Pattern-Hard c words**:
Pattern-"ow" words: how growl downtown towel   climb castle country
Pattern-ble words: bubble marble stable tremble   comb cotton crocodile
Pattern-dle words: bundle candle puddle middle

Lesson 26

50

receive ceiling monkey valley honey toe foe doe boat road toast throat groan soap loaf loaves candy candies chilly sunny empty copy copies puppies blow grow bowl slow Europe feud feudal few argue rescue view review face place mice fence since cents juice city blew chew flew grew soup group wound true glue due sue avenue choose food broom troop loose shoot soon tooth noon push bushes fault sauce cause pause author stood wood took shook jaw straw crawl awful fancy center peace voice recess loud house shout mouth found ounce how growl downtown towel climb castle comb country cotton crocodile bubble marble stable tremble bundle candle puddle middle **live give hear busy truth shoe sew door floor both easy**

Lesson 27 - Review

Pattern-"oi" words: soil coin join point poison
Pattern-"oy" words: toy enjoy royal destroy   **Pattern-fle words**: rifle ruffle sniffle
Pattern-ple words: apple dimple sample   **Pattern-kle words**: ankle buckle tickle
Pattern-gle words: giggle jungle single struggle   sparkle twinkle

Lesson 28

Pattern-"er" words: jerk verse nerve perch stem winter upper answer
Pattern-"ir" words: bird thirst shirt chirp third
Pattern-tle words: battle bottle little settle   **Pattern-stle words**: wrestle hustle whistle
Pattern-zle words: puzzle fizzle   Sight words: woman women

Lesson 29

Pattern-"ur" words: hurt burn nurse turn **Pattern-"ar" words**: beggar cellar dollar collar
Pattern-"or" words: worm work worship world word worth worse doctor
Pattern-"ear" words: earn learn search heard earth early   Sight words: whose pint
Know your complete address and complete phone number

Lesson 30

Pattern-Days of the week: Sunday Monday Tuesday Wednesday Thursday Friday Saturday   Sight words: which care pair pear tear wear bear
Pattern-Color words: yellow orange red pink purple blue green brown black white
 Know your complete address and complete telephone number

Lesson 31

Pattern-Months of the year: January February March April May June July August September October November December
Know your complete address and complete phone number   Sight words: heaven hell devil Satan God lamb Bible Almighty Holy Spirit parents animals

Lesson 32

51

soil coin join point poison toy enjoy royal destroy apple dimple sample giggle jungle single struggle riffle ruffle sniffle ankle buckle tickle sparkle twinkle jerk verse nerve perch stern winter upper answer bird thirst shirt chirp third battle bottle little settle puzzle fizzle wrestle hustle whistle hurt burn nurse turn beggar cellar dollar collar worm work worship world word worth worse doctor earn learn search heard earth early Sunday Monday Tuesday Wednesday Thursday Friday Saturday yellow orange red pink purple blue green brown black white January February March April May June July August September October November December **hell heaven devil Satan God lamb Bible Almighty Holy Spirit animals parents which care pair pear tear wear bear whose pint woman women**

Lesson 33 - Review

Pattern-"g" words: strange huge change
Pattern-"dge" words: badge judge dodge budge pledge
Pattern-r-controlled words: farm hard large heart force horse morning starfish popcorn airport   **Pattern-"tch" words**: ditch stretch sketch catch scratch crutch

Lesson 34

Pattern-Number words: eleven twelve thirteen fourteen fifteen sixteen seventeen eighteen nineteen twenty   **Pattern-Contractions**: you're they're we're doesn't didn't won't that's he's I've you'll she'll   <u>Sight words</u>: fought bought thought

Lesson 35

Sunday Monday Tuesday Wednesday Thursday Friday Saturday January February March April May June July August September October November December ditch stretch sketch catch scratch crutch strange huge change badge judge dodge budge pledge farm hard large heart force horse morning starfish popcorn airport eleven twelve thirteen fourteen fifteen sixteen seventeen eighteen nineteen twenty you're they're we're doesn't didn't won't that's he's I've you'll she'll **heaven hell devil Satan God lamb Bible Almighty Holy Spirit animals which pear tear wear bear whose pint woman women hear busy truth shoe sew care pair sweat bread head read dead these those through gone to door floor both easy live almost own friend sugar their father people during too none laughed president pretty girl boy else use no know much such children every color Jesus Christ sure fought bought thought parents could should would won again against once hour over come some something only very really ever our goes does where were have there here been many any give minute shall pull full what who want said was they enough are of off because you your says**

Lesson 36 - Review

52

Worksheet 1

Name_____

Directions: A. **Repeat and Write**: Repeat each word after your teacher and then write the word carefully in <u>print</u>. Check the spelling and memorize how the letters fit together to make each word.

B. **Alphabetize in Print or Cursive**: (Your teacher will tell you which style to use.) Alphabetize the list **in each group** by numbering the bubbles that follow each word. <u>Groups are separated by dotted lines</u>. After all the bubbles have been numbered, write the words alphabetically in the right hand column.

Repeat and Write		**Alphabetize in Print or Cursive**
1. spelling	⃝	1. _____
2. was	⃝	2. _____
3. off	⃝	3. _____
4. test	⃝	1. _____
5. are	⃝	2. _____
6. spell	⃝	3. _____
7. said	⃝	1. _____
8. of	⃝	2. _____
9. they	⃝	3. _____
10. because	⃝	4. _____

Write your teacher's name 3 times.   _____

_____   _____

53

Worksheet 1-B   Name _____

Directions: A. **Flip and Write**: Flip your paper over and look at the first spelling word. Flip
             the page back and write it in <u>print or cursive</u> in the left column below.
             (Your teacher will tell you which style to use.)

             B. **CAPITAL PRINT**: Print the spelling words using CAPITAL letters in the right
             column below. Check each word to make sure you have printed it correctly.

Flip and Write   **CAPITAL PRINT**

1. _____   1. _____

2. _____   2. _____

3. _____   3. _____

4. _____   4. _____

5. _____   5. _____

6. _____   6. _____

7. _____   7. _____

8. _____   8. _____

9. _____   9. _____

10. _____   10. _____

Write your first name 3 times.   Write your middle name 3 times.   Write your last name 3 times.

_____   _____   _____

_____   _____   _____

_____   _____   _____

Worksheet 2

Name_____

What is the pattern? _____

Repeat and Write		**Alphabetize in Print or Cursive**

1. jam _____ ○ 1. _____

2. set _____ ○ 2. _____

3. got _____ ○ 3. _____

4. cab _____ ○ 4. _____

5. met _____ ○ 5. _____

---

6. sit _____ ○ 1. _____

7. bug _____ ○ 2. _____

8. win _____ ○ 3. _____

9. pen _____ ○ 4. _____

10. hum _____ ○ 5. _____

---

11. nut _____ ○ 1. _____

12. pin _____ ○ 2. _____

13. box _____ ○ 3. _____

14. log _____ ○ 4. _____

15. has _____ ○ 5. _____

In the left column mark the short vowels with a **breve**.

Write your teacher's name.

_____

Name _____

Flip and Write   **CAPITAL PRINT**

1. _____   1. _____

2. _____   2. _____

3. _____   3. _____

4. _____   4. _____

5. _____   5. _____

6. _____   6. _____

7. _____   7. _____

8. _____   8. _____

9. _____   9. _____

10. _____   10. _____

11. _____   11. _____

12. _____   12. _____

13. _____   13. _____

14. _____   14. _____

15. _____   15. _____

Write: your first name   your middle name   your last name

_____   _____   _____

spelling   test   said   was   because

_____   _____   _____

Worksheet 3

What is the pattern? _____

Repeat and Write		Alphabetize in Print or Cursive

Repeat and Write

1. shed _____ ○
2. when _____ ○
3. plus _____ ○
4. whip _____ ○
5. shut _____ ○
6. chin _____ ○

Alphabetize in Print or Cursive

1. _____
2. _____
3. _____
4. _____
5. _____
6. _____

---

7. them _____ ○
8. blot _____ ○
9. chop _____ ○
10. slim _____ ○
11. glad _____ ○
12. sled _____ ○
13. clap _____ ○

1. _____
2. _____
3. _____
4. _____
5. _____
6. _____
7. _____

---

14. flag _____ ○
15. that _____ ○
16. club _____ ○
17. flip _____ ○
18. glob _____ ○
19. plan _____ ○
20. blab _____ ○

1. _____
2. _____
3. _____
4. _____
5. _____
6. _____
7. _____

In the left column mark the short vowels with a **breve**. In the right column circle the beginning blends.

Name _____

Flip and Write	**CAPITAL PRINT**
1. _____	1. _____
2. _____	2. _____
3. _____	3. _____
4. _____	4. _____
5. _____	5. _____
6. _____	6. _____
7. _____	7. _____
8. _____	8. _____
9. _____	9. _____
10. _____	10. _____
11. _____	11. _____
12. _____	12. _____
13. _____	13. _____
14. _____	14. _____
15. _____	15. _____
16. _____	16. _____
17. _____	17. _____
18. _____	18. _____
19. _____	19. _____
20. _____	20. _____

Write 2 times:

you   your   says   goes   does

_____   _____   _____   _____   _____

_____   _____   _____   _____   _____

Worksheet 4

Name_____

What is the pattern? _____

Repeat and Write		**Alphabetize in Print or Cursive**

1. drop   _____ ⟳   1. _____

2. smog   _____ ⟳   2. _____

3. crop   _____ ⟳   3. _____

4. brim   _____ ⟳   4. _____

5. from   _____ ⟳   5. _____

6. grin   _____ ⟳   6. _____

---

7. trip   _____ ⟳   1. _____

8. scan   _____ ⟳   2. _____

9. fret   _____ ⟳   3. _____

10. skin   _____ ⟳   4. _____

11. here   _____ ⟳   5. _____

12. there   _____ ⟳   6. _____

13. prop   _____ ⟳   7. _____

---

14. prim   _____ ⟳   1. _____

15. where   _____ ⟳   2. _____

16. scab   _____ ⟳   3. _____

17. were   _____ ⟳   4. _____

18. skid   _____ ⟳   5. _____

19. crab   _____ ⟳   6. _____

20. smug   _____ ⟳   7. _____

In the left column mark the short vowels with a **breve**. In the right column circle the beginning blends.

Name _____

Flip and Write	**CAPITAL PRINT**
1. _____	1. _____
2. _____	2. _____
3. _____	3. _____
4. _____	4. _____
5. _____	5. _____
6. _____	6. _____
7. _____	7. _____
8. _____	8. _____
9. _____	9. _____
10. _____	10. _____
11. _____	11. _____
12. _____	12. _____
13. _____	13. _____
14. _____	14. _____
15. _____	15. _____
16. _____	16. _____
17. _____	17. _____
18. _____	18. _____
19. _____	19. _____
20. _____	20. _____

Write 2 times:

brag   grab   drum   trot   have

_____   _____   _____   _____   _____

_____   _____   _____   _____   _____

Worksheet 5

Name_____

What is the pattern? _____

Repeat and Write		Alphabetize in Print or Cursive

1. scrub _____ ◯   1. _____

2. throb _____ ◯   2. _____

3. span _____ ◯   3. _____

4. quit _____ ◯   4. _____

5. spin _____ ◯   5. _____

6. swim _____ ◯   6. _____

- -

7. strap _____ ◯   1. _____

8. shrub _____ ◯   2. _____

9. twig _____ ◯   3. _____

10. stem _____ ◯   4. _____

11. snap _____ ◯   5. _____

12. school _____ ◯   6. _____

13. quiz _____ ◯   7. _____

- -

14. scrap _____ ◯   1. _____

15. step _____ ◯   2. _____

16. shrug _____ ◯   3. _____

17. swam _____ ◯   4. _____

18. split _____ ◯   5. _____

19. twin _____ ◯   6. _____

20. snug _____ ◯   7. _____

In the left column mark the short vowels with a **breve**. In the right column circle the beginning blends.

Name _____

Flip and Write

1. _____
2. _____
3. _____
4. _____
5. _____
6. _____
7. _____
8. _____
9. _____
10. _____
11. _____
12. _____
13. _____
14. _____
15. _____
16. _____
17. _____
18. _____
19. _____
20. _____

CAPITAL PRINT

1. _____
2. _____
3. _____
4. _____
5. _____
6. _____
7. _____
8. _____
9. _____
10. _____
11. _____
12. _____
13. _____
14. _____
15. _____
16. _____
17. _____
18. _____
19. _____
20. _____

Write 2 times:

spry   sprig   squid   squad   strip

_____   _____   _____   _____   _____

_____   _____   _____   _____   _____

Worksheet 6

Name_____

What is the pattern? _____

Repeat and Write		**Alphabetize in Print or Cursive**

1. gulf _____ ◯ 1. _____

2. self _____ ◯ 2. _____

3. told _____ ◯ 3. _____

4. cold _____ ◯ 4. _____

5. held _____ ◯ 5. _____

6. grand _____ ◯ 6. _____

- -

7. brush _____ ◯ 1. _____

8. squish _____ ◯ 2. _____

9. with _____ ◯ 3. _____

10. milk _____ ◯ 4. _____

11. flash _____ ◯ 5. _____

12. island _____ ◯ 6. _____

13. psalm _____ ◯ 7. _____

- -

14. wrist _____ ◯ 1. _____

15. must _____ ◯ 2. _____

16. fond _____ ◯ 3. _____

17. fast _____ ◯ 4. _____

18. cloth _____ ◯ 5. _____

19. calm _____ ◯ 6. _____

20. shelf _____ ◯ 7. _____

In the left column mark the short vowels with a **breve** and the long vowels with a **macron**. In the middle column circle the silent letters in island and psalm. In the right column circle the final blends.

63

Worksheet 6-B   Name _____

Flip and Write   ### CAPITAL PRINT

1. _____   1. _____
2. _____   2. _____
3. _____   3. _____
4. _____   4. _____
5. _____   5. _____
6. _____   6. _____
7. _____   7. _____
8. _____   8. _____
9. _____   9. _____
10. _____   10. _____
11. _____   11. _____
12. _____   12. _____
13. _____   13. _____
14. _____   14. _____
15. _____   15. _____
16. _____   16. _____
17. _____   17. _____
18. _____   18. _____
19. _____   19. _____
20. _____   20. _____

Write 2 times:

any   many   been   bath   because

_____   _____   _____   _____   _____

_____   _____   _____   _____   _____

Worksheet 7 Review

Name_____

Repeat and Write   **Repeat and Write**

1. spelling _____
2. test _____
3. jam _____
4. set _____
5. sit _____
6. got _____
7. hum _____
8. cab _____
9. met _____
10. win _____
11. box _____
12. bug _____
13. has _____
14. pen _____
15. pin _____
16. nut _____
17. log _____
18. chin _____
19. chop _____
20. shut _____
21. shed _____
22. them _____
23. that _____
24. when _____
25. whip _____
26. blot _____
27. blab _____
28. clap _____
29. club _____
30. flag _____

31. flip _____
32. glad _____
33. glob _____
34. plan _____
35. plus _____
36. sled _____
37. slim _____
38. brim _____
39. brag _____
40. crab _____
41. crop _____
42. drum _____
43. drop _____
44. fret _____
45. from _____
46. grin _____
47. grab _____
48. prop _____
49. prim _____
50. trip _____
51. trot _____
52. scab _____
53. scan _____
54. skid _____
55. skin _____
56. smog _____
57. smug _____
58. snap _____
59. snug _____
60. span _____

Worksheet 7-B Review

Name_____

Repeat and Write   **Repeat and Write**

61.	spin	_____	91.	grand	_____
62.	step	_____	92.	must	_____
63.	stem	_____	93.	wrist	_____
64.	swam	_____	94.	brush	_____
65.	swim	_____	95.	flash	_____
66.	quit	_____	96.	with	_____
67.	quiz	_____	97.	cloth	_____
68.	twig	_____	98.	said	_____
69.	twin	_____	99.	was	_____
70.	school	_____	100.	they	_____
71.	scrap	_____	101.	are	_____
72.	scrub	_____	102.	of	_____
73.	shrug	_____	103.	off	_____
74.	shrub	_____	104.	because	_____
75.	split	_____	105.	you	_____
76.	spry	_____	106.	your	_____
77.	sprig	_____	107.	says	_____
78.	squad	_____	108.	goes	_____
79.	squid	_____	109.	does	_____
80.	strap	_____	110.	where	_____
81.	strip	_____	111.	were	_____
82.	throb	_____	112.	have	_____
83.	held	_____	113.	there	_____
84.	told	_____	114.	here	_____
85.	self	_____	115.	been	_____
86.	shelf	_____	116.	many	_____
87.	milk	_____	117.	any	_____
88.	calm	_____	118.		_____
89.	psalm	_____	119.		_____
90.	island	_____	120.		_____

Worksheet 8

What is the pattern? _____

	Repeat and Write		**Alphabetize in Print or Cursive**

1. scalp _____ ◯ 1. _____

2. crisp _____ ◯ 2. _____

3. swift _____ ◯ 3. _____

4. stomp _____ ◯ 4. _____

5. exact _____ ◯ 5. _____

6. went _____ ◯ 6. _____

---

7. mask _____ ◯ 1. _____

8. melt _____ ◯ 2. _____

9. gulp _____ ◯ 3. _____

10. kept _____ ◯ 4. _____

11. yelp _____ ◯ 5. _____

12. plant _____ ◯ 6. _____

13. brisk _____ ◯ 7. _____

---

14. desk _____ ◯ 1. _____

15. bump _____ ◯ 2. _____

16. slept _____ ◯ 3. _____

17. lift _____ ◯ 4. _____

18. grasp _____ ◯ 5. _____

19. wilt _____ ◯ 6. _____

20. fact _____ ◯ 7. _____

In the left column mark the short vowels with a **breve**. In the right column circle the final blends.

Name _____

Flip and Write

1. _____
2. _____
3. _____
4. _____
5. _____
6. _____
7. _____
8. _____
9. _____
10. _____
11. _____
12. _____
13. _____
14. _____
15. _____
16. _____
17. _____
18. _____
19. _____
20. _____

CAPITAL PRINT

1. _____
2. _____
3. _____
4. _____
5. _____
6. _____
7. _____
8. _____
9. _____
10. _____
11. _____
12. _____
13. _____
14. _____
15. _____
16. _____
17. _____
18. _____
19. _____
20. _____

Write 2 times:

what	want	who	print	felt
_____	_____	_____	_____	_____
_____	_____	_____	_____	_____

Worksheet 9

What is the pattern? _____

Repeat and Write		**Alphabetize in Print or Cursive**

Repeat and Write

1. bang _____

2. bring _____

3. drank _____

4. bank _____

5. honk _____

6. belong _____

○ ○ ○ ○ ○ ○

Alphabetize in Print or Cursive

1. _____

2. _____

3. _____

4. _____

5. _____

6. _____

---

7. lung _____

8. think _____

9. skunk _____

10. strong _____

11. song _____

12. shrink _____

13. dunk _____

○ ○ ○ ○ ○ ○ ○

1. _____

2. _____

3. _____

4. _____

5. _____

6. _____

7. _____

---

14. spring _____

15. rang _____

16. spunk _____

17. conk _____

18. hang _____

19. stung _____

20. wing _____

○ ○ ○ ○ ○ ○ ○

1. _____

2. _____

3. _____

4. _____

5. _____

6. _____

7. _____

In the left column circle the vowel and the **ng** final blend. In the right column circle the vowel and the **nk** final blend.

Worksheet 9-B

Name _____

Flip and Write

CAPITAL PRINT

1. _____ 1. _____
2. _____ 2. _____
3. _____ 3. _____
4. _____ 4. _____
5. _____ 5. _____
6. _____ 6. _____
7. _____ 7. _____
8. _____ 8. _____
9. _____ 9. _____
10. _____ 10. _____
11. _____ 11. _____
12. _____ 12. _____
13. _____ 13. _____
14. _____ 14. _____
15. _____ 15. _____
16. _____ 16. _____
17. _____ 17. _____
18. _____ 18. _____
19. _____ 19. _____
20. _____ 20. _____

Write 2 times:

only   very   really   ever   our

_____ _____ _____ _____ _____

_____ _____ _____ _____ _____

70

Worksheet 10

Name_____

What is the pattern? _____

Repeat and Write		**Alphabetize in Print or Cursive**

1. class _____ ○ 1. _____

2. cross _____ ○ 2. _____

3. cell _____ ○ 3. _____

4. miss _____ ○ 4. _____

5. cliff _____ ○ 5. _____

6. bless _____ ○ 6. _____

- -

7. yell _____ ○ 1. _____

8. bell _____ ○ 2. _____

9. pass _____ ○ 3. _____

10. thrill _____ ○ 4. _____

11. smell _____ ○ 5. _____

12. puff _____ ○ 6. _____

13. grass _____ ○ 7. _____

- -

14. well _____ ○ 1. _____

15. glass _____ ○ 2. _____

16. small _____ ○ 3. _____

17. bluff _____ ○ 4. _____

18. stuff _____ ○ 5. _____

19. buzz _____ ○ 6. _____

20. fuzz _____ ○ 7. _____

In the left column mark the short vowels with a **breve**. In the right column circle the final blends.

71

Name _____

Flip and Write	**CAPITAL PRINT**
1. _____	1. _____
2. _____	2. _____
3. _____	3. _____
4. _____	4. _____
5. _____	5. _____
6. _____	6. _____
7. _____	7. _____
8. _____	8. _____
9. _____	9. _____
10. _____	10. _____
11. _____	11. _____
12. _____	12. _____
13. _____	13. _____
14. _____	14. _____
15. _____	15. _____
16. _____	16. _____
17. _____	17. _____
18. _____	18. _____
19. _____	19. _____
20. _____	20. _____

Write 2 times:

sell   dress   sniff   shall   pull   full

_____   _____   _____   _____   _____   _____

_____   _____   _____   _____   _____   _____

Worksheet 11

Name_____

What is the pattern? _____

Repeat and Write		**Alphabetize in Print or Cursive**
1. too	○	1. _____
2. seven	○	2. _____
3. to	○	3. _____
4. once	○	4. _____
5. two	○	5. _____
6. minute	○	6. _____

- -

7. one	○	1. _____
8. three	○	2. _____
9. against	○	3. _____
10. hour	○	4. _____
11. five	○	5. _____
12. won	○	6. _____
13. four	○	7. _____

- -

14. should	○	1. _____
15. could	○	2. _____
16. would	○	3. _____
17. over	○	4. _____
18. some	○	5. _____
19. eight	○	6. _____
20. again	○	7. _____

Homophones are words that sound alike, but they are spelled differently. There are three homophones in the first group and a pair of homophones in the second group. In the left column circle all of them.

Name _____

Flip and Write   **CAPITAL PRINT**

1. _____   1. _____
2. _____   2. _____
3. _____   3. _____
4. _____   4. _____
5. _____   5. _____
6. _____   6. _____
7. _____   7. _____
8. _____   8. _____
9. _____   9. _____
10. _____   10. _____
11. _____   11. _____
12. _____   12. _____
13. _____   13. _____
14. _____   14. _____
15. _____   15. _____
16. _____   16. _____
17. _____   17. _____
18. _____   18. _____
19. _____   19. _____
20. _____   20. _____

Write 2 times:

come   something   ten   nine   six

_____   _____   _____   _____   _____

_____   _____   _____   _____   _____

Worksheet 12

Name_____

What is the pattern? _____

Repeat and Write		**Alphabetize in Print or Cursive**
1. wash	⟶ ○	1. _____
2. talk	○	2. _____
3. about	○	3. _____
4. alike	○	4. _____
5. walk	○	5. _____
6. war	○	6. _____

---

7. alive	○	1. _____
8. above	○	2. _____
9. chalk	○	3. _____
10. water	○	4. _____
11. ahead	○	5. _____
12. around	○	6. _____
13. along	○	7. _____

---

14. halt	○	1. _____
15. away	○	2. _____
16. ward	○	3. _____
17. across	○	4. _____
18. awhile	○	5. _____
19. watch	○	6. _____
20. afraid	○	7. _____

In the left column circle all words that start with an **a**. In the right column circle the words that have **al** in the middle.

Name _____

Flip and Write   **CAPITAL PRINT**

Flip and Write	Capital Print
1. _____	1. _____
2. _____	2. _____
3. _____	3. _____
4. _____	4. _____
5. _____	5. _____
6. _____	6. _____
7. _____	7. _____
8. _____	8. _____
9. _____	9. _____
10. _____	10. _____
11. _____	11. _____
12. _____	12. _____
13. _____	13. _____
14. _____	14. _____
15. _____	15. _____
16. _____	16. _____
17. _____	17. _____
18. _____	18. _____
19. _____	19. _____
20. _____	20. _____

Write 2 times:

asleep   amaze   war   minute   hour

_____ _____ _____ _____ _____

_____ _____ _____ _____ _____

Worksheet 13 Review

Repeat and Write **Print or Cursive**

1. because _____
2. use _____
3. no _____
4. know _____
5. much _____
6. such _____
7. any _____
8. many _____
9. here _____
10. there _____
11. have _____
12. were _____
13. where _____
14. does _____
15. goes _____
16. our _____
17. are _____
18. really _____
19. very _____
20. only _____
21. been _____
22. some _____
23. who _____
24. come _____

1. _____
2. _____
3. _____
4. _____
5. _____
6. _____
7. _____
8. _____
9. _____
10. _____
11. _____
12. _____
13. _____
14. _____
15. _____
16. _____
17. _____
18. _____
19. _____
20. _____
21. _____
22. _____
23. _____
24. _____

Worksheet 13-B

	Repeat and Write	**Print or Cursive**
25. over	_____	25. _____
26. says	_____	26. _____
27. your	_____	27. _____
28. you	_____	28. _____
29. off	_____	29. _____
30. of	_____	30. _____
31. ever	_____	31. _____
32. they	_____	32. _____
33. was	_____	33. _____
34. said	_____	34. _____
35. want	_____	35. _____
36. what	_____	36. _____
37. full	_____	37. _____
38. pull	_____	38. _____
39. could	_____	39. _____
40. should	_____	40. _____
41. would	_____	41. _____
42. won	_____	42. _____
43. again	_____	43. _____
44. against	_____	44. _____
45. once	_____	45. _____
46. hour	_____	46. _____
47. minute	_____	47. _____
48. shall	_____	48. _____

Worksheet 14

What is the pattern? _____

Repeat and Write		Alphabetize in Print or Cursive

Repeat and Write   **Alphabetize in Print or Cursive**

1. quarter _____   ○   1. _____
2. dime _____   ○   2. _____
3. nickel _____   ○   3. _____
4. dollar _____   ○   4. _____
5. money _____   ○   5. _____
6. penny _____   ○   6. _____

- -

7. people _____   ○   1. _____
8. pretty _____   ○   2. _____
9. other _____   ○   3. _____
10. pennies _____   ○   4. _____
11. nothing _____   ○   5. _____
12. children _____   ○   6. _____
13. mother _____   ○   7. _____

- -

14. sister _____   ○   1. _____
15. another _____   ○   2. _____
16. father _____   ○   3. _____
17. brother _____   ○   4. _____
18. every _____   ○   5. _____
19. month _____   ○   6. _____
20. else _____   ○   7. _____

In the left column circle all words where the **o** says /ŭ/ for the middle sound.

Name _____

Flip and Write   **CAPITAL PRINT**

1. _____   1. _____
2. _____   2. _____
3. _____   3. _____
4. _____   4. _____
5. _____   5. _____
6. _____   6. _____
7. _____   7. _____
8. _____   8. _____
9. _____   9. _____
10. _____   10. _____
11. _____   11. _____
12. _____   12. _____
13. _____   13. _____
14. _____   14. _____
15. _____   15. _____
16. _____   16. _____
17. _____   17. _____
18. _____   18. _____
19. _____   19. _____
20. _____   20. _____

Write 2 times:

girl   boy   smother   really

_____   _____   _____   _____

_____   _____   _____   _____

Worksheet 15 Review

Name _____

Repeat and Write   **Repeat and Write**

1. scalp _____
2. felt _____
3. desk _____
4. stomp _____
5. slept _____
6. hang _____
7. bring _____
8. strong _____
9. belong _____
10. lung _____
11. buzz _____
12. cell _____
13. sell _____
14. yell _____
15. warm _____
16. walk _____
17. wash _____
18. water _____
19. watch _____
20. awhile _____
21. asleep _____
22. ahead _____
23. crisp _____
24. exact _____
25. swift _____
26. went _____
27. bless _____
28. bank _____
29. think _____
30. honk _____

31. skunk _____
32. cliff _____
33. grass _____
34. two _____
35. four _____
36. seven _____
37. eight _____
38. about _____
39. alike _____
40. alive _____
41. along _____
42. away _____
43. above _____
44. across _____
45. amaze _____
46. afraid _____
47. around _____
48. other _____
49. mother _____
50. brother _____
51. another _____
52. nothing _____
53. something _____
54. girl _____
55. boy _____
56. every _____
57. pretty _____
58. won _____
59. again _____
60. against _____

Worksheet 15-B Review

Name_____

Repeat and Write		**Repeat and Write**	
61. hour	_____	91. what	_____
62. minute	_____	92. who	_____
63. shall	_____	93. want	_____
64. else	_____	94. our	_____
65. use	_____	95. any	_____
66. no	_____	96. many	_____
67. know	_____	97. one	_____
68. dollar	_____	98. three	_____
69. quarter	_____	99. five	_____
70. dime	_____	100. six	_____
71. nickel	_____	101. chalk	_____
72. penny	_____	102. talk	_____
73. pennies	_____	103. smell	_____
74. money	_____	104. shrink	_____
75. month	_____	105. dress	_____
76. father	_____	106. spring	_____
77. children	_____	107. says	_____
78. sister	_____	108. been	_____
79. should	_____	109. because	_____
80. could	_____	110. are	_____
81. would	_____	111. kept	_____
82. once	_____	112. come	_____
83. people	_____	113. some	_____
84. to	_____	114. only	_____
85. too	_____	115. very	_____
86. much	_____	116. really	_____
87. such	_____	117. ever	_____
88. over	_____	118. where	_____
89. pull	_____	119. were	_____
90. full	_____	120. they	_____

Worksheet 16

Name_____

What is the pattern? _____

Repeat and Write		**Alphabetize in Print or Cursive**

1. pencil _____ ◯ 1. _____

2. sudden _____ ◯ 2. _____

3. selfish _____ ◯ 3. _____

4. basket _____ ◯ 4. _____

5. dentist _____ ◯ 5. _____

6. enough _____ ◯ 6. _____

- -

7. truly _____ ◯ 1. _____

8. tiny _____ ◯ 2. _____

9. pony _____ ◯ 3. _____

10. lady _____ ◯ 4. _____

11. zero _____ ◯ 5. _____

12. visit _____ ◯ 6. _____

13. lazy _____ ◯ 7. _____

- -

14. Jesus _____ ◯ 1. _____

15. sunset _____ ◯ 2. _____

16. sure _____ ◯ 3. _____

17. crazy _____ ◯ 4. _____

18. color _____ ◯ 5. _____

19. magnet _____ ◯ 6. _____

20. Christ _____ ◯ 7. _____

In the left column divide all words between the syllables. In the middle column and working with only the ODD numbered words, put a **breve** above the short vowel sounds and a **macron** above the long vowel sounds.

Name _____

Flip and Write	**CAPITAL PRINT**

1. _____ 1. _____
2. _____ 2. _____
3. _____ 3. _____
4. _____ 4. _____
5. _____ 5. _____
6. _____ 6. _____
7. _____ 7. _____
8. _____ 8. _____
9. _____ 9. _____
10. _____ 10. _____
11. _____ 11. _____
12. _____ 12. _____
13. _____ 13. _____
14. _____ 14. _____
15. _____ 15. _____
16. _____ 16. _____
17. _____ 17. _____
18. _____ 18. _____
19. _____ 19. _____
20. _____ 20. _____

Write 2 times:

icy   cabin   contest   baby

_____   _____   _____   _____

_____   _____   _____   _____

Worksheet 17

What is the pattern? _____

Repeat and Write		**Alphabetize in Print or Cursive**
1. pancake	_____ ○	1. _____
2. sunshine	_____ ○	2. _____
3. mistake	_____ ○	3. _____
4. locate	_____ ○	4. _____
5. invite	_____ ○	5. _____
6. nicely	_____ ○	6. _____

- -

7. beside	_____ ○	1. _____
8. before	_____ ○	2. _____
9. admire	_____ ○	3. _____
10. dislike	_____ ○	4. _____
11. friend	_____ ○	5. _____
12. plane	_____ ○	6. _____
13. their	_____ ○	7. _____

- -

14. state	_____ ○	1. _____
15. sugar	_____ ○	2. _____
16. cube	_____ ○	3. _____
17. escape	_____ ○	4. _____
18. decide	_____ ○	5. _____
19. pavement	_____ ○	6. _____
20. write	_____ ○	7. _____

In the left column divide all words between the syllables. In the middle column and
working with only the EVEN numbered words, put a **breve** above the short vowels, and a
macron above the long vowels, and cross out the silent **e**.

Name _____

Flip and Write	**CAPITAL PRINT**
1. _____	1. _____
2. _____	2. _____
3. _____	3. _____
4. _____	4. _____
5. _____	5. _____
6. _____	6. _____
7. _____	7. _____
8. _____	8. _____
9. _____	9. _____
10. _____	10. _____
11. _____	11. _____
12. _____	12. _____
13. _____	13. _____
14. _____	14. _____
15. _____	15. _____
16. _____	16. _____
17. _____	17. _____
18. _____	18. _____
19. _____	19. _____
20. _____	20. _____

Write 2 times:

ate   same   hope   cone

_____   _____   _____   _____

_____   _____   _____   _____

Worksheet 18

Name_____

What is the pattern? _____

	Repeat and Write		**Alphabetize in Print or Cursive**
1. president	_____	◯	1. _____
2. dryer	_____	◯	2. _____
3. nighttime	_____	◯	3. _____
4. pie	_____	◯	4. _____
5. chief	_____	◯	5. _____
6. high	_____	◯	6. _____

- -

7. piece	_____	◯	1. _____
8. believe	_____	◯	2. _____
9. frightened	_____	◯	3. _____
10. flying	_____	◯	4. _____
11. lightning	_____	◯	5. _____
12. laughed	_____	◯	6. _____
13. mightier	_____	◯	7. _____

- -

14. reply	_____	◯	1. _____
15. thief	_____	◯	2. _____
16. brightly	_____	◯	3. _____
17. lie	_____	◯	4. _____
18. niece	_____	◯	5. _____
19. own	_____	◯	6. _____
20. belief	_____	◯	7. _____

In the left column divide all words between the syllables. In the middle column circle the **igh** words. In the right column circle all the **ie** words that have a long /ē/ sound.

Name _____

Flip and Write

1. _____
2. _____
3. _____
4. _____
5. _____
6. _____
7. _____
8. _____
9. _____
10. _____
11. _____
12. _____
13. _____
14. _____
15. _____
16. _____
17. _____
18. _____
19. _____
20. _____

CAPITAL PRINT

1. _____
2. _____
3. _____
4. _____
5. _____
6. _____
7. _____
8. _____
9. _____
10. _____
11. _____
12. _____
13. _____
14. _____
15. _____
16. _____
17. _____
18. _____
19. _____
20. _____

Write 2 times:

why   higher   mightily   almost

_____   _____   _____   _____

_____   _____   _____   _____

Worksheet 19

What is the pattern? _____

Repeat and Write		**Alphabetize in Print or Cursive**
1. neighbor	⬤	1. _____
2. daily	⬤	2. _____
3. through	⬤	3. _____
4. mailman	⬤	4. _____
5. sailor	⬤	5. _____
6. sprain	⬤	6. _____

7. weigh	⬤	1. _____
8. praying	⬤	2. _____
9. these	⬤	3. _____
10. payment	⬤	4. _____
11. during	⬤	5. _____
12. gone	⬤	6. _____
13. survey	⬤	7. _____

14. played	⬤	1. _____
15. stay	⬤	2. _____
16. wait	⬤	3. _____
17. weight	⬤	4. _____
18. obey	⬤	5. _____
19. fail	⬤	6. _____
20. none	⬤	7. _____

In the left column divide all words between the syllables and circle the **eigh** words. In the middle column circle all of the **ay** words. In the right column circle all of the **ey** words.

Name _____

Flip and Write

1. _____
2. _____
3. _____
4. _____
5. _____
6. _____
7. _____
8. _____
9. _____
10. _____
11. _____
12. _____
13. _____
14. _____
15. _____
16. _____
17. _____
18. _____
19. _____
20. _____

CAPITAL PRINT

1. _____
2. _____
3. _____
4. _____
5. _____
6. _____
7. _____
8. _____
9. _____
10. _____
11. _____
12. _____
13. _____
14. _____
15. _____
16. _____
17. _____
18. _____
19. _____
20. _____

Write 2 times:

hey   clay   those   rain

_____   _____   _____   _____

_____   _____   _____   _____

Worksheet 20

What is the pattern? _____

	Repeat and Write		**Alphabetize in Print or Cursive**

1. steel _____   ○   1. _____

2. steal _____   ○   2. _____

3. head _____   ○   3. _____

4. week _____   ○   4. _____

5. weak _____   ○   5. _____

6. sweat _____   ○   6. _____

----

7. feet _____   ○   1. _____

8. feat _____   ○   2. _____

9. leaf _____   ○   3. _____

10. read _____   ○   4. _____

11. see _____   ○   5. _____

12. sea _____   ○   6. _____

13. leaves _____   ○   7. _____

----

14. meet _____   ○   1. _____

15. meat _____   ○   2. _____

16. dead _____   ○   3. _____

17. freedom _____   ○   4. _____

18. seem _____   ○   5. _____

19. seam _____   ○   6. _____

20. bread _____   ○   7. _____

In the left column circle two pairs of homophones for each group. In the middle column mark the vowels for the homophones. In the right column circle the words where the **ea** is a short /ĕ/ sound and mark the **e** with a **breve**.

Name _____

Flip and Write	**CAPITAL PRINT**
1. _____	1. _____
2. _____	2. _____
3. _____	3. _____
4. _____	4. _____
5. _____	5. _____
6. _____	6. _____
7. _____	7. _____
8. _____	8. _____
9. _____	9. _____
10. _____	10. _____
11. _____	11. _____
12. _____	12. _____
13. _____	13. _____
14. _____	14. _____
15. _____	15. _____
16. _____	16. _____
17. _____	17. _____
18. _____	18. _____
19. _____	19. _____
20. _____	20. _____

Write 2 times:

tease   plead   speech   sweet

_____ _____ _____ _____

_____ _____ _____ _____

Worksheet 21 Review

Name_____

Repeat and Write

1. pencil _____
2. visit _____
3. sudden _____
4. sunset _____
5. magnet _____
6. basket _____
7. pony _____
8. lazy _____
9. tiny _____
10. icy _____
11. ate _____
12. locate _____
13. mistake _____
14. pancake _____
15. same _____
16. hope _____
17. invite _____
18. admire _____
19. cone _____
20. pavement _____
21. nicely _____
22. decide _____
23. contest _____
24. dentist _____
25. selfish _____
26. cabin _____
27. crazy _____
28. truly _____
29. lady _____
30. baby _____

31. zero _____
32. plane _____
33. before _____
34. sunshine _____
35. cube _____
36. dislike _____
37. beside _____
38. escape _____
39. write _____
40. state _____
41. lightning _____
42. mightily _____
43. high _____
44. mightier _____
45. brightly _____
46. higher _____
47. frightened _____
48. nighttime _____
49. flying _____
50. dryer _____
51. pie _____
52. lie _____
53. sailor _____
54. rain _____
55. fail _____
56. mailman _____
57. sprain _____
58. obey _____
59. hey _____
60. survey _____

Name_____

Repeat and Write

		Repeat and Write

61. tease _____ 91. seem _____

62. weak _____ 92. meet _____

63. feat _____ 93. freedom _____

64. steal _____ 94. feet _____

65. sea _____ 95. see _____

66. leaf _____ 96. speech _____

67. leaves _____ 97. sweet _____

68. plead _____ 98. bread _____

69. meat _____ 99. dead _____

70. seam _____ 100. sweat _____

71. why _____ 101. read _____

72. reply _____ 102. head _____

73. chief _____ 103. these _____

74. niece _____ 104. those _____

75. piece _____ 105. through _____

76. belief _____ 106. gone _____

77. thief _____ 107. none _____

78. believe _____ 108. during _____

79. wait _____ 109. president _____

80. daily _____ 110. laughed _____

81. praying _____ 111. almost _____

82. clay _____ 112. color _____

83. stay _____ 113. own _____

84. payment _____ 114. friend _____

85. played _____ 115. sugar _____

86. weigh _____ 116. their _____

87. weight _____ 117. enough _____

88. neighbor _____ 118. sure _____

89. week _____ 119. Jesus _____

90. steel _____ 120. Christ _____

Worksheet 22

What is the pattern? _____

Name_____

Repeat and Write		Alphabetize in Print or Cursive

Repeat and Write

1. receive _____ ○
2. ceiling _____ ○
3. monkey _____ ○
4. valley _____ ○
5. honey _____ ○
6. toe _____ ○

Alphabetize in Print or Cursive

1. _____
2. _____
3. _____
4. _____
5. _____
6. _____

----

7. doe _____ ○
8. foe _____ ○
9. candy _____ ○
10. candies _____ ○
11. boat _____ ○
12. copy _____ ○
13. copies _____ ○

1. _____
2. _____
3. _____
4. _____
5. _____
6. _____
7. _____

----

14. groan _____ ○
15. road _____ ○
16. toast _____ ○
17. loaf _____ ○
18. loaves _____ ○
19. empty _____ ○
20. puppies _____ ○

1. _____
2. _____
3. _____
4. _____
5. _____
6. _____
7. _____

In the left column circle the words that end in **ey**. In the right column circle the words where the **y** was **changed to i** and **es was added**.

Name _____

Flip and Write

1. _____
2. _____
3. _____
4. _____
5. _____
6. _____
7. _____
8. _____
9. _____
10. _____
11. _____
12. _____
13. _____
14. _____
15. _____
16. _____
17. _____
18. _____
19. _____
20. _____

CAPITAL PRINT

1. _____
2. _____
3. _____
4. _____
5. _____
6. _____
7. _____
8. _____
9. _____
10. _____
11. _____
12. _____
13. _____
14. _____
15. _____
16. _____
17. _____
18. _____
19. _____
20. _____

Write 2 times:

soap   throat   chilly   sunny

_____   _____   _____   _____

_____   _____   _____   _____

Worksheet 23

Name_____

What is the pattern? _____

Repeat and Write		**Alphabetize in Print or Cursive**
1. blow	○	1. _____
2. grow	○	2. _____
3. bowl	○	3. _____
4. slow	○	4. _____
5. argue	○	5. _____
6. rescue	○	6. _____

7. Europe	○	1. _____
8. feudal	○	2. _____
9. feud	○	3. _____
10. few	○	4. _____
11. view	○	5. _____
12. review	○	6. _____
13. mice	○	7. _____

14. face	○	1. _____
15. juice	○	2. _____
16. place	○	3. _____
17. fence	○	4. _____
18. since	○	5. _____
19. cents	○	6. _____
20. city	○	7. _____

In the left column circle the words that have a **soft c** sound. In the middle column circle the words where the **eu** makes the /ū/ sound. In the right column circle where the **ue** makes the /ū/ sound.

Name _____

Flip and Write

1. _____
2. _____
3. _____
4. _____
5. _____
6. _____
7. _____
8. _____
9. _____
10. _____
11. _____
12. _____
13. _____
14. _____
15. _____
16. _____
17. _____
18. _____
19. _____
20. _____

CAPITAL PRINT

1. _____
2. _____
3. _____
4. _____
5. _____
6. _____
7. _____
8. _____
9. _____
10. _____
11. _____
12. _____
13. _____
14. _____
15. _____
16. _____
17. _____
18. _____
19. _____
20. _____

Write 2 times:

door   floor   both   easy

_____   _____   _____   _____

_____   _____   _____   _____

Worksheet 24

Name_____

What is the pattern? _____

Repeat and Write		**Alphabetize in Print or Cursive**
1. true _____	○	1. _____
2. glue _____	○	2. _____
3. due _____	○	3. _____
4. sue _____	○	4. _____
5. avenue _____	○	5. _____
6. truth _____	○	6. _____
7. food _____	○	1. _____
8. broom _____	○	2. _____
9. troop _____	○	3. _____
10. choose _____	○	4. _____
11. loose _____	○	5. _____
12. shoot _____	○	6. _____
13. soon _____	○	7. _____
14. tooth _____	○	1. _____
15. blew _____	○	2. _____
16. chew _____	○	3. _____
17. flew _____	○	4. _____
18. grew _____	○	5. _____
19. shoe _____	○	6. _____
20. sew _____	○	7. _____

In the left column circle the words that have a **double o**. In the middle column circle the words where the **ew** makes the /ü/ sound. In the right column circle where the **ue** makes the /ü/ sound.

Name _____

Flip and Write

CAPITAL PRINT

1. _____
2. _____
3. _____
4. _____
5. _____
6. _____
7. _____
8. _____
9. _____
10. _____
11. _____
12. _____
13. _____
14. _____
15. _____
16. _____
17. _____
18. _____
19. _____
20. _____

1. _____
2. _____
3. _____
4. _____
5. _____
6. _____
7. _____
8. _____
9. _____
10. _____
11. _____
12. _____
13. _____
14. _____
15. _____
16. _____
17. _____
18. _____
19. _____
20. _____

Write 2 times:

noon   soup   group   wound

_____   _____   _____   _____

_____   _____   _____   _____

Worksheet 25

What is the pattern? _____

Repeat and Write   **Alphabetize in Print or Cursive**

1. fault _____ ○ 1. _____
2. sauce _____ ○ 2. _____
3. cause _____ ○ 3. _____
4. pause _____ ○ 4. _____
5. author _____ ○ 5. _____
6. hear _____ ○ 6. _____

----

7. push _____ ○ 1. _____
8. bushes _____ ○ 2. _____
9. jaw _____ ○ 3. _____
10. straw _____ ○ 4. _____
11. crawl _____ ○ 5. _____
12. awful _____ ○ 6. _____
13. busy _____ ○ 7. _____

----

14. took _____ ○ 1. _____
15. shook _____ ○ 2. _____
16. wood _____ ○ 3. _____
17. stood _____ ○ 4. _____
18. voice _____ ○ 5. _____
19. peace _____ ○ 6. _____
20. recess _____ ○ 7. _____

In the left column circle the words that have a **soft c** sound. In the middle column circle the words spelled with **au**. In the right column circle the words spelled with **aw**.

Name _____

Flip and Write	**CAPITAL PRINT**
1. _____	1. _____
2. _____	2. _____
3. _____	3. _____
4. _____	4. _____
5. _____	5. _____
6. _____	6. _____
7. _____	7. _____
8. _____	8. _____
9. _____	9. _____
10. _____	10. _____
11. _____	11. _____
12. _____	12. _____
13. _____	13. _____
14. _____	14. _____
15. _____	15. _____
16. _____	16. _____
17. _____	17. _____
18. _____	18. _____
19. _____	19. _____
20. _____	20. _____

Write 2 times:

give   live   fancy   center

_____   _____   _____   _____

_____   _____   _____   _____

Worksheet 26

What is the pattern? _____

Repeat and Write		**Alphabetize in Print or Cursive**

1. climb   _____   ◯   1. _____

2. bubble   _____   ◯   2. _____

3. loud   _____   ◯   3. _____

4. bundle   _____   ◯   4. _____

5. house   _____   ◯   5. _____

6. marble   _____   ◯   6. _____

---

7. castle   _____   ◯   1. _____

8. candle   _____   ◯   2. _____

9. shout   _____   ◯   3. _____

10. stable   _____   ◯   4. _____

11. comb   _____   ◯   5. _____

12. puddle   _____   ◯   6. _____

13. country   _____   ◯   7. _____

---

14. mouth   _____   ◯   1. _____

15. middle   _____   ◯   2. _____

16. cotton   _____   ◯   3. _____

17. found   _____   ◯   4. _____

18. tremble   _____   ◯   5. _____

19. ounce   _____   ◯   6. _____

20. crocodile   _____   ◯   7. _____

In the left column divide the syllables. In the right column circle the **hard c** words.

Name _____

Flip and Write   **CAPITAL PRINT**

1. _____   1. _____
2. _____   2. _____
3. _____   3. _____
4. _____   4. _____
5. _____   5. _____
6. _____   6. _____
7. _____   7. _____
8. _____   8. _____
9. _____   9. _____
10. _____   10. _____
11. _____   11. _____
12. _____   12. _____
13. _____   13. _____
14. _____   14. _____
15. _____   15. _____
16. _____   16. _____
17. _____   17. _____
18. _____   18. _____
19. _____   19. _____
20. _____   20. _____

Write 2 times:

how   growl   downtown   towel

_____   _____   _____   _____

_____   _____   _____   _____

Worksheet 27 Review

Name_____

Repeat and Write

1. receive _____
2. ceiling _____
3. monkey _____
4. valley _____
5. honey _____
6. toe _____
7. doe _____
8. foe _____
9. boat _____
10. road _____
11. toast _____
12. throat _____
13. groan _____
14. soap _____
15. loaf _____
16. loaves _____
17. candy _____
18. candies _____
19. chilly _____
20. sunny _____
21. empty _____
22. copy _____
23. copies _____
24. puppies _____
25. bowl _____
26. slow _____
27. Europe _____
28. feud _____
29. feudal _____
30. blow _____

Repeat and Write

31. grow _____
32. argue _____
33. rescue _____
34. few _____
35. view _____
36. review _____
37. face _____
38. mice _____
39. fence _____
40. since _____
41. cents _____
42. juice _____
43. place _____
44. city _____
45. fancy _____
46. center _____
47. peace _____
48. voice _____
49. recess _____
50. group _____
51. wound _____
52. soup _____
53. chew _____
54. grew _____
55. flew _____
56. blew _____
57. sue _____
58. true _____
59. glue _____
60. avenue _____

Name_____

Repeat and Write   **Repeat and Write**

61. due _____   91. ounce _____
62. tooth _____   92. how _____
63. noon _____   93. growl _____
64. choose _____   94. towel _____
65. food _____   95. downtown _____
66. broom _____   96. cotton _____
67. troop _____   97. country _____
68. loose _____   98. comb _____
69. shoot _____   99. climb _____
70. soon _____   100. castle _____
71. bushes _____   101. crocodile _____
72. push _____   102. live _____
73. sauce _____   103. give _____
74. cause _____   104. hear _____
75. pause _____   105. door _____
76. author _____   106. floor _____
77. fault _____   107. easy _____
78. shook _____   108. both _____
79. took _____   109. truth _____
80. straw _____   110. sew _____
81. crawl _____   111. busy _____
82. awful _____   112. show _____
83. jaw _____   113. bundle _____
84. wood _____   114. tremble _____
85. stood _____   115. stable _____
86. loud _____   116. marble _____
87. house _____   117. middle _____
88. shout _____   118. puddle _____
89. mouth _____   119. candle _____
90. found _____   120. bubble _____

Worksheet 28

What is the pattern? _____

Repeat and Write   **Alphabetize in Print or Cursive**

1. rifle _____ ◯   1. _____

2. apple _____ ◯   2. _____

3. ankle _____ ◯   3. _____

4. soil _____ ◯   4. _____

5. giggle _____ ◯   5. _____

6. coin _____ ◯   6. _____

- -

7. sample _____ ◯   1. _____

8. ruffle _____ ◯   2. _____

9. join _____ ◯   3. _____

10. buckle _____ ◯   4. _____

11. jungle _____ ◯   5. _____

12. dimple _____ ◯   6. _____

13. tickle _____ ◯   7. _____

- -

14. single _____ ◯   1. _____

15. sniffle _____ ◯   2. _____

16. sparkle _____ ◯   3. _____

17. twinkle _____ ◯   4. _____

18. struggle _____ ◯   5. _____

19. point _____ ◯   6. _____

20. poison _____ ◯   7. _____

In the left column divide the syllables. In the right column circle the **oi** words.

Name _____

Flip and Write	**CAPITAL PRINT**
1. _____	1. _____
2. _____	2. _____
3. _____	3. _____
4. _____	4. _____
5. _____	5. _____
6. _____	6. _____
7. _____	7. _____
8. _____	8. _____
9. _____	9. _____
10. _____	10. _____
11. _____	11. _____
12. _____	12. _____
13. _____	13. _____
14. _____	14. _____
15. _____	15. _____
16. _____	16. _____
17. _____	17. _____
18. _____	18. _____
19. _____	19. _____
20. _____	20. _____

Write 2 times:

toy   enjoy   royal   destroy

_____ _____ _____ _____

_____ _____ _____ _____

Worksheet 29

What is the pattern? _____

	Repeat and Write		**Alphabetize in Print or Cursive**

Repeat and Write

1. battle _____ ◯   1. _____
2. bird _____ ◯   2. _____
3. jerk _____ ◯   3. _____
4. bottle _____ ◯   4. _____
5. verse _____ ◯   5. _____
6. thirst _____ ◯   6. _____

7. little _____ ◯   1. _____
8. shirt _____ ◯   2. _____
9. settle _____ ◯   3. _____
10. nerve _____ ◯   4. _____
11. perch _____ ◯   5. _____
12. stern _____ ◯   6. _____
13. winter _____ ◯   7. _____

14. wrestle _____ ◯   1. _____
15. chirp _____ ◯   2. _____
16. hustle _____ ◯   3. _____
17. third _____ ◯   4. _____
18. whistle _____ ◯   5. _____
19. upper _____ ◯   6. _____
20. answer _____ ◯   7. _____

In the left column divide the syllables. In the right column circle the **ir** words.

Name _____

Flip and Write   **CAPITAL PRINT**

1. _____   1. _____
2. _____   2. _____
3. _____   3. _____
4. _____   4. _____
5. _____   5. _____
6. _____   6. _____
7. _____   7. _____
8. _____   8. _____
9. _____   9. _____
10. _____   10. _____
11. _____   11. _____
12. _____   12. _____
13. _____   13. _____
14. _____   14. _____
15. _____   15. _____
16. _____   16. _____
17. _____   17. _____
18. _____   18. _____
19. _____   19. _____
20. _____   20. _____

Write 2 times:

fizzle   puzzle   woman   women

_____   _____   _____   _____

_____   _____   _____   _____

Worksheet 30

Name_____

What is the pattern? _____

Repeat and Write		**Alphabetize in Print or Cursive**
1. whose	_____ ◯	1. _____
2. pint	_____ ◯	2. _____
3. beggar	_____ ◯	3. _____
4. cellar	_____ ◯	4. _____
5. dollar	_____ ◯	5. _____
6. collar	_____ ◯	6. _____

7. earn	_____ ◯	1. _____
8. learn	_____ ◯	2. _____
9. search	_____ ◯	3. _____
10. heard	_____ ◯	4. _____
11. early	_____ ◯	5. _____
12. earth	_____ ◯	6. _____
13. doctor	_____ ◯	7. _____

14. worth	_____ ◯	1. _____
15. world	_____ ◯	2. _____
16. worse	_____ ◯	3. _____
17. hurt	_____ ◯	4. _____
18. burn	_____ ◯	5. _____
19. nurse	_____ ◯	6. _____
20. turn	_____ ◯	7. _____

On Worksheet 30-C write your complete name, complete address, and complete phone number. Make sure you know how to write this information for the spelling test this week.

Name _____

Flip and Write

1. _____
2. _____
3. _____
4. _____
5. _____
6. _____
7. _____
8. _____
9. _____
10. _____
11. _____
12. _____
13. _____
14. _____
15. _____
16. _____
17. _____
18. _____
19. _____
20. _____

CAPITAL PRINT

1. _____
2. _____
3. _____
4. _____
5. _____
6. _____
7. _____
8. _____
9. _____
10. _____
11. _____
12. _____
13. _____
14. _____
15. _____
16. _____
17. _____
18. _____
19. _____
20. _____

Write 2 times:

worm   work   worship   word

_____   _____   _____   _____

_____   _____   _____   _____

Write your complete address.

_____

First Name   Middle Name   Last Name

_____

Complete Address (DO NOT abbreviate.)

_____

City   (comma)   State   Zip Code

Write your complete phone number.

_____

(Area Code)   Prefix   -   Suffix

Write your complete address.

_____

First Name   Middle Name   Last Name

_____

Complete Address (DO NOT abbreviate.)

_____

City   (comma)   State   Zip Code

Write your complete phone number.

_____

(Area Code)   Prefix   -   Suffix

Worksheet 31

Name_____

What is the pattern? _____

Repeat and Write		**Alphabetize in Print or Cursive**

Repeat and Write

1. Wednesday _____ ◯ 1. _____
2. Tuesday _____ ◯ 2. _____
3. Monday _____ ◯ 3. _____
4. Thursday _____ ◯ 4. _____
5. Friday _____ ◯ 5. _____
6. Saturday _____ ◯ 6. _____

----

7. Sunday _____ ◯ 1. _____
8. bear _____ ◯ 2. _____
9. wear _____ ◯ 3. _____
10. tear _____ ◯ 4. _____
11. pear _____ ◯ 5. _____
12. pair _____ ◯ 6. _____
13. care _____ ◯ 7. _____

----

14. which _____ ◯ 1. _____
15. brown _____ ◯ 2. _____
16. black _____ ◯ 3. _____
17. blue _____ ◯ 4. _____
18. orange _____ ◯ 5. _____
19. yellow _____ ◯ 6. _____
20. purple _____ ◯ 7. _____

On Worksheet 31-C write your complete name, complete address, and complete phone number. Make sure you know how to write this information for the spelling test this week.

Name _____

Flip and Write   **CAPITAL PRINT**

1. _____   1. _____
2. _____   2. _____
3. _____   3. _____
4. _____   4. _____
5. _____   5. _____
6. _____   6. _____
7. _____   7. _____
8. _____   8. _____
9. _____   9. _____
10. _____   10. _____
11. _____   11. _____
12. _____   12. _____
13. _____   13. _____
14. _____   14. _____
15. _____   15. _____
16. _____   16. _____
17. _____   17. _____
18. _____   18. _____
19. _____   19. _____
20. _____   20. _____

Write 2 times:

green   red   pink   white

_____   _____   _____   _____

_____   _____   _____   _____

Worksheet 32

Name_____

What is the pattern? _____

Repeat and Write		**Alphabetize in Print or Cursive**

1. heaven _____ ⚫ 1. _____

2. God _____ ⚫ 2. _____

3. Almighty _____ ⚫ 3. _____

4. Holy _____ ⚫ 4. _____

5. Spirit _____ ⚫ 5. _____

6. Bible _____ ⚫ 6. _____

- -

7. September _____ ⚫ 1. _____

8. November _____ ⚫ 2. _____

9. December _____ ⚫ 3. _____

10. devil _____ ⚫ 4. _____

11. Satan _____ ⚫ 5. _____

12. hell _____ ⚫ 6. _____

13. January _____ ⚫ 7. _____

- -

14. February _____ ⚫ 1. _____

15. April _____ ⚫ 2. _____

16. August _____ ⚫ 3. _____

17. October _____ ⚫ 4. _____

18. lamb _____ ⚫ 5. _____

19. parents _____ ⚫ 6. _____

20. animals _____ ⚫ 7. _____

On Worksheet 32-C write your complete name, complete address, and complete phone number. Make sure you know how to write this information for the spelling test this week.

Name _____

Flip and Write	**CAPITAL PRINT**

1. _____   1. _____

2. _____   2. _____

3. _____   3. _____

4. _____   4. _____

5. _____   5. _____

6. _____   6. _____

7. _____   7. _____

8. _____   8. _____

9. _____   9. _____

10. _____   10. _____

11. _____   11. _____

12. _____   12. _____

13. _____   13. _____

14. _____   14. _____

15. _____   15. _____

16. _____   16. _____

17. _____   17. _____

18. _____   18. _____

19. _____   19. _____

20. _____   20. _____

Write 2 times:

March   May   June   July

_____   _____   _____   _____

_____   _____   _____   _____

Worksheet 33 Review

Name_____

Repeat and Write   **Repeat and Write**

1. soil _____
2. coin _____
3. join _____
4. point _____
5. poison _____
6. toy _____
7. enjoy _____
8. royal _____
9. destroy _____
10. rifle _____
11. ruffle _____
12. sniffle _____
13. ankle _____
14. buckle _____
15. tickle _____
16. tickle _____
17. sparkle _____
18. twinkle _____
19. apple _____
20. dimple _____
21. sample _____
22. giggle _____
23. jungle _____
24. single _____
25. struggle _____
26. winter _____
27. upper _____
28. answer _____
29. jerk _____
30. verse _____

31. nerve _____
32. stern _____
33. perch _____
34. fizzle _____
35. puzzle _____
36. bird _____
37. thirst _____
38. shirt _____
39. chirp _____
40. third _____
41. battle _____
42. bottle _____
43. settle _____
44. little _____
45. hustle _____
46. whistle _____
47. wrestle _____
48. beggar _____
49. cellar _____
50. dollar _____
51. collar _____
52. worm _____
53. work _____
54. worship _____
55. world _____
56. word _____
57. worth _____
58. worse _____
59. doctor _____
60. burn _____

Name_____

Repeat and Write

61. nurse _____
62. turn _____
63. hurt _____
64. earn _____
65. learn _____
66. search _____
67. heard _____
68. earth _____
69. early _____
70. blue _____
71. green _____
72. brown _____
73. black _____
74. yellow _____
75. orange _____
76. red _____
77. pink _____
78. purple _____
79. white _____
80. which _____
81. care _____
82. pair _____
83. pear _____
84. bear _____
85. tear _____
86. wear _____
87. women _____
88. woman _____
89. pint _____
90. January _____

Repeat and Write

91. February _____
92. March _____
93. April _____
94. May _____
95. June _____
96. July _____
97. August _____
98. September _____
99. October _____
100. November _____
101. December _____
102. Monday _____
103. Tuesday _____
104. Wednesday _____
105. Thursday _____
106. Friday _____
107. Saturday _____
108. Sunday _____
109. whose _____
110. lamb _____
111. hell _____
112. devil _____
113. Satan _____
114. animals _____
115. parents _____
116. God _____
117. Almighty _____
118. Holy _____
119. Bible _____
120. Spirit _____

Worksheet 34

What is the pattern? _____

Repeat and Write		Alphabetize in Print or Cursive

1. ditch   _____ ○   1. _____

2. large   _____ ○   2. _____

3. badge   _____ ○   3. _____

4. stretch _____ ○   4. _____

5. heart   _____ ○   5. _____

6. judge   _____ ○   6. _____

- -

7. sketch   _____ ○   1. _____

8. change   _____ ○   2. _____

9. strange _____ ○   3. _____

10. huge   _____ ○   4. _____

11. catch   _____ ○   5. _____

12. dodge   _____ ○   6. _____

13. force   _____ ○   7. _____

- -

14. horse   _____ ○   1. _____

15. scratch _____ ○   2. _____

16. budge   _____ ○   3. _____

17. morning _____ ○   4. _____

18. airport _____ ○   5. _____

19. crutch _____ ○   6. _____

20. pledge _____ ○   7. _____

In the left column circle the words with the **dge** sound. In the right column circle the words with the **tch** sound.

Name _____

Flip and Write   **CAPITAL PRINT**

1. _____   1. _____
2. _____   2. _____
3. _____   3. _____
4. _____   4. _____
5. _____   5. _____
6. _____   6. _____
7. _____   7. _____
8. _____   8. _____
9. _____   9. _____
10. _____   10. _____
11. _____   11. _____
12. _____   12. _____
13. _____   13. _____
14. _____   14. _____
15. _____   15. _____
16. _____   16. _____
17. _____   17. _____
18. _____   18. _____
19. _____   19. _____
20. _____   20. _____

Write 2 times:

farm   hard   starfish   popcorn

_____   _____   _____   _____

_____   _____   _____   _____

Name_____

What is the pattern? _____

Repeat and Write		**Alphabetize in Print or Cursive**

1. fought _____ ○ 1. _____

2. bought _____ ○ 2. _____

3. thought _____ ○ 3. _____

4. eleven _____ ○ 4. _____

5. twelve _____ ○ 5. _____

6. thirteen _____ ○ 6. _____

- -

7. eighteen _____ ○ 1. _____

8. twenty _____ ○ 2. _____

9. fifteen _____ ○ 3. _____

10. they're _____ ○ 4. _____

11. we're _____ ○ 5. _____

12. doesn't _____ ○ 6. _____

13. didn't _____ ○ 7. _____

- -

14. won't _____ ○ 1. _____

15. that's _____ ○ 2. _____

16. he's _____ ○ 3. _____

17. I've _____ ○ 4. _____

18. you'll _____ ○ 5. _____

19. she'll _____ ○ 6. _____

20. you're _____ ○ 7. _____

In the right column circle the silent **gh** in the words. Check your work to make sure you placed the apostrophe correctly in the contraction words.

Name _____

Flip and Write

1. _____
2. _____
3. _____
4. _____
5. _____
6. _____
7. _____
8. _____
9. _____
10. _____
11. _____
12. _____
13. _____
14. _____
15. _____
16. _____
17. _____
18. _____
19. _____
20. _____

CAPITAL PRINT

1. _____
2. _____
3. _____
4. _____
5. _____
6. _____
7. _____
8. _____
9. _____
10. _____
11. _____
12. _____
13. _____
14. _____
15. _____
16. _____
17. _____
18. _____
19. _____
20. _____

Write 2 times:

fourteen   sixteen   seventeen   nineteen

_____   _____   _____   _____

_____   _____   _____   _____

Worksheet 36 Review

Name_____

Repeat and Write   **Repeat and Write**

#	Word		#	Word	
1.	Sunday	_____	31.	sixteen	_____
2.	Monday	_____	32.	seventeen	_____
3.	Tuesday	_____	33.	eighteen	_____
4.	Wednesday	_____	34.	nineteen	_____
5.	Thursday	_____	35.	twenty	_____
6.	Friday	_____	36.	you're	_____
7.	Saturday	_____	37.	they're	_____
8.	January	_____	38.	we're	_____
9.	February	_____	39.	doesn't	_____
10.	March	_____	40.	didn't	_____
11.	April	_____	41.	won't	_____
12.	May	_____	42.	that's	_____
13.	June	_____	43.	he's	_____
14.	July	_____	44.	I've	_____
15.	August	_____	45.	you'll	_____
16.	September	_____	46.	she'll	_____
17.	October	_____	47.	strange	_____
18.	November	_____	48.	huge	_____
19.	December	_____	49.	change	_____
20.	ditch	_____	50.	badge	_____
21.	stretch	_____	51.	judge	_____
22.	sketch	_____	52.	dodge	_____
23.	catch	_____	53.	budge	_____
24.	scratch	_____	54.	pledge	_____
25.	crutch	_____	55.	farm	_____
26.	eleven	_____	56.	hard	_____
27.	twelve	_____	57.	large	_____
28.	thirteen	_____	58.	heart	_____
29.	fourteen	_____	59.	force	_____
30.	fifteen	_____	60.	morning	_____

Repeat and Write   **Repeat and Write**

61. horse _____   92. sweat _____
62. starfish _____   93. bread _____
63. popcorn _____   34. head _____
64. airport _____   95. read _____
65. hell _____   96. dead _____
66. heaven _____   97. these _____
67. devil _____   98. those _____
68. Satan _____   99. through _____
69. God _____   100. during _____
70. lamb _____   101. gone _____
71. Bible _____   102. door _____
72. Almighty _____   103. floor _____
73. Holy _____   104. both _____
74. Spirit _____   105. easy _____
75. animals _____   106. live _____
76. which _____   107. almost _____
77. pear _____   108. own _____
78. tear _____   109. friend _____
79. wear _____   110. sugar _____
80. bear _____   111. their _____
81. whose _____   112. father _____
82. pint _____   113. people _____
83. woman _____   114. none _____
84. women _____   115. laughed _____
85. hear _____   116. president _____
86. busy _____   117. pretty _____
87. truth _____   118. girl _____
88. shoe _____   119. boy _____
89. sew _____   120. else _____
90. care _____   121. enough _____
91. pair _____   122. use _____

Name_____

Repeat and Write		**Repeat and Write**	
123. says	_____	154. our	_____
124. no	_____	155. goes	_____
125. much	_____	156. does	_____
126. such	_____	157. where	_____
127. children	_____	158. were	_____
128. every	_____	159. have	_____
129. color	_____	160. there	_____
130. Jesus	_____	161. here	_____
131. Christ	_____	162. been	_____
132. sure	_____	163. many	_____
133. fought	_____	164. any	_____
134. bought	_____	165. give	_____
135. thought	_____	166. minute	_____
136. parents	_____	167. to	_____
137. could	_____	168. too	_____
138. should	_____	169. shall	_____
139. would	_____	170. pull	_____
140. won	_____	171. full	_____
141. again	_____	172. who	_____
142. against	_____	173. want	_____
143. once	_____	174. said	_____
144. hour	_____	175. was	_____
145. over	_____	176. they	_____
146. come	_____	177. what	_____
147. some	_____	178. are	_____
148. something	_____	179. of	_____
149. only	_____	180. off	_____
150. very	_____	181. because	_____
151. really	_____	182. you	_____
152. says	_____	183. your	_____
153. ever	_____		